CAN
HOLDING IN
A FART
KILL YOU?

Can Holding in a Fart Kill You?

Over 150 Curious Questions & Intriguing Answers

Andrew Thompson

Ulysses Press

Published in the U.S. by
ULYSSES PRESS
P.O. Box 3440
Berkeley, CA 94703
www.ulyssespress.com

ISBN: 978-1-61243-475-9
Library of Congress Control Number 2015937154

10 9 8 7 6 5 4 3

Printed in Canada by Marquis Book Printing

Managing Editor: Claire Chun
Editor: Kathy Kaiser
Proofreader: Lauren Harrison
Layout: Lindsay Tamura
Front cover design: what!design @ whatweb.com
Front cover artwork: © Hein Nouwens/shutterstock.com
Back cover artwork: bottle © Ruslan Semichev/shutterstock.com;
    popcorn © Ruslan Semichev/shutterstock.com; dinosaur ©
    para/shutterstock.com; dog © warat42/shutterstock.com
Interior artwork: see page 205

Distributed by Publishers Group West

To Hugo

Contents

CAN THE GREAT WALL OF CHINA BE SEEN FROM SPACE?

It is commonly said that the Great Wall of China is the only human-made structure that can be seen with the naked eye from space or the moon. This assertion has been perpetuated as a question in the board game Trivial Pursuit. It has also been included in schoolbooks across the world, and was stated as true by the Ed Harris character in the 1998 movie *The Truman Show*. In addition, Richard Halliburton's *Second Book of Marvels* makes this claim (despite the fact that the book was published in 1938, before space exploration had begun).

One school of thought is that the claim was made to convey the enormous scale of the wall and the vastness of human achievement in building it. It is now accepted that the statement is false.

From a low orbit of Earth (up to about 200 miles), many human-made objects can be seen with the naked eye. Highways, airports, buildings, and ships, as well as the Great Wall, can be seen. The wall's width ranges from about 15 to 30 feet, but when dust storms hit it, it becomes more visible at this close range because of the combined size of the wall and the dust turbulence.

But no human-made structures are visible with the naked eye above an altitude of a few thousand miles, and certainly not from the moon. The moon is around 240,000 miles away, and from there, entire continents and oceans are barely visible without mechanical assistance. These facts have been confirmed beyond any doubt by a number of astronauts.

WHY IS THE OCEAN SALTY?

The oceans of the world cover around 70 percent of the Earth's surface. They are filled with salt, and—despite much mythology on the topic—it is not commonly known why.

There are many constituents of seawater, but the primary chemicals are sodium and chloride. These are the components of salt and account for the salty taste of the ocean.

All water contains some salt, but the salts in seawater are increased by the gradual dissolution of the Earth's crust and the erosion of rocks and mountains. Rainwater is slightly

acidic from the carbon dioxide it absorbs from the air. When rain falls to the ground, its carbonic acid erodes rocks and forms ions (mainly sodium and chloride ions). Rainwater and rivers then transport these minerals from rocks and soil to the sea, increasing the salt content.

The salt content of the ocean is also augmented by evaporation. The sun evaporates freshwater from the surface of the ocean to the atmosphere, leaving the salts behind. This process is known as the hydrologic cycle. Because only freshwater is evaporated and rain brings more salts to the sea, as time passes, the oceans are actually becoming saltier. In fact, it is thought that the oceans contain 50 million billion tons of salt and that if all the salt was removed from the world's oceans and spread across the land, the layer would be approximately 180 yards (165 meters) thick.

The salinity of different oceans varies according to location. In areas of high water temperature, the evaporation rate is increased, leading to saltier water. Oceans that are remote from land also receive a smaller influx of freshwater, which increases their salinity. In polar areas where the salt is diluted by melting ice and excess rain, salinity tends to be low. The saltiest areas of all the oceans are the Red Sea and the Persian Gulf, where evaporation is at its highest.

WHAT CAUSES HEADACHES?

Medically known as *cephalalgia*, headaches have a multitude of causes, such as sleep deprivation, dehydration, stress, eyestrain, sinus pain, and muscle tension.

Where there is a disorder or pain somewhere in the body, nociceptors, which are pain-sensitive receptors at the ends of nerve fibers, are activated. The nociceptors send a signal to the brain, which the brain interprets as pain. A headache results. The area of the head where the pain is felt depends on the location of the activated nociceptors.

When the brain is alerted to pain, it also produces a number of chemicals, including serotonin, that act to reduce pain. However, the release of these chemicals can cause a swelling of blood vessels in the brain, making the blood  vessels tender. The swollen vessels then irritate the nerve fibers that surround them in the head. These nerve fibers send messages to the trigeminal system, which is an area of the brain dealing with pain in the face and head. This can cause the headache to worsen.

Medication to alleviate the effects of a headache works best if taken early. Once the pathways for the pain signals, transmitted by the nerves, are fully activated, it is more difficult to prevent the signals and thus reduce the headache.

HOW DO GUN SILENCERS WORK?

A silencer, also known as a suppressor, is a device that is attached to the end of a gun barrel to reduce the amount of noise that is generated when the gun is fired.

When the trigger of a loaded gun is pulled, gunpowder is ignited, which creates high-pressure hot gas. This expanding gas forces the bullet down the barrel of the gun, resulting in a loud noise as the bullet exits.

The silencer is usually a cylindrical piece of metal that is screwed on to the end of the barrel, although it can be attached to the gun as a permanent fixture. It is composed of a group of baffles inside an expansion chamber. The baffles are hollow plates that divert the flow of the gas within the expansion chamber, which is larger in diameter than the barrel of the gun. This allows the gas to cool and reduce in energy. As the gas leaves the expansion chamber, its pressure and speed are less. This greatly reduces the sound when the bullet and gas are released. In this way, the silencer has a similar effect as the muffler of a car.

Silencers are most effective when attached to small-caliber weapons, especially when subsonic bullets are used. These are bullets that make less noise, as they travel slower than the speed of sound. Some silencers use small quantities of oil or water to cool the gas and reduce its pressure. These are known as "wet" suppressors.

The term *silencer* is actually a misnomer, as a silencer only decreases the noise created—it doesn't eliminate it. Silencers are often depicted incorrectly in movies and on television shows. In these fictional portrayals, virtually no sound is heard when a gun with a silencer is fired.

The commercial silencer was invented by Hiram Maxim and first sold in 1902 in the United States. The legality of the silencer varies widely in different parts of the world.

? WHAT IS THE ORIGIN OF THE SCOTTISH KILT?

One of the most widely recognized traditional garments for men, the kilt is associated with the Scottish Highlands. The word derives from *kjilt*, a Norse word meaning "pleated." The *kjilt* was a similar item of apparel worn by Viking settlers.

The great kilt dates back to at least 1600 in Scotland, when it was worn by military troops. It was a large garment (around 5 yards long), worn by draping it across the shoulder and over the body. The lower portion was gathered in pleats and secured with a belt. It provided ideal protection from the cold and the elements.

The origin of the smaller and more convenient modern kilt has been the topic of heated debate. Many say that it was invented in 1720 by Thomas Rawlinson, who was English. He owned a charcoal production plant in Scotland and had the great kilt tailored to make it more practical for working men. However, it is now known that the modern kilt was worn before Rawlinson, and one, which resides at the Scottish Tartans Society, has been dated to 1692. By the mid-1700s, the modern kilt had become popular throughout the Highlands and parts of the Lowlands. When parts of the Scottish military were deployed abroad, the different regiments were assigned different tartans as a means of identification (although some say the tartan was used to distinguish different clans of people in Scotland).

In 1746, the English government controlled Scotland. Wary of a Highland uprising, the English government prohibited Highlanders from possessing arms. The Dress Act was also enacted, which outlawed all aspects of Highland attire, including the kilt. This ban lasted for 35 years, during which time many Highland customs were lost. Upper-class Scots set up societies advocating the resurgence of ancient Highland dress. The Celtic Society of Edinburgh encouraged Lowlanders to join them, and the movement gained momentum. In 1822, King George IV visited Scotland and wore a kilt. Queen Victoria then promoted the wearing of kilts, and the style became widespread.

Today, kilts are commonly worn at Scottish formal occasions, although some continue to wear the kilt daily.

WHAT MAKES POPCORN POP?

First developed by Native Americans, popcorn has been popularly sold in movie theaters since 1912. The first commercial popcorn machine was invented in 1885 in Chicago.

Popcorn is an ancient type of maize that is specially cultivated to increase the corn's ability to pop. In fact, popcorn is the only type of corn that pops, and the name comes from the Middle English word *poppe*, which means "explosive sound."

Popcorn is able to pop because its tiny kernels contain a small amount of water (at least 14 percent is required).

Unlike most corn, popcorn's kernel is encased inside a hard, waterproof outer shell. When heated with oil to around 350°F (175°C), the water evaporates and expands, creating high pressure, which is unable to escape. This pressure builds and eventually forces the outer casing to explode, turning the kernel inside out. The sudden explosion changes the starch inside the kernel into a light foam, and gives cooked popcorn its peculiar appearance.

Popcorn coated with butter is the most popular variety, and the kernels that fail to pop are known as "old maids."

WHAT CAUSES A "STITCH" DURING EXERCISE?

A stitch, formally known as exercise-related transient abdominal pain (or ETAP), is a sharp, stabbing pain that commonly occurs just under the rib cage during exercise. A stitch can also result in a stabbing pain in the shoulder blade, which is thought to be a pain referral site for the abdomen.

It is not entirely clear what causes a stitch. It was traditionally thought that exercise makes internal organs, such as the liver, pull on the ligaments that connect the gut to the diaphragm, resulting in stress, or a stitch. Others believed that a stitch is caused by blood being redirected away from the diaphragm to the limb muscles used during exercise.

It is now commonly thought that a stitch results from the irritation of two layers of the membrane lining that is inside the wall of the abdomen. The two layers are separated by lubricating fluid, which allows them to move against each other without friction. Scientists believe that a stitch is the pain that occurs when the two layers rub against each other and create friction. This is thought to be caused by either a reduction in the fluid that lubricates the two layers or by a distended stomach forcing the layers close together. This friction is generally more likely to occur during exercises that involve an up-and-down action, such as running or jumping.

Eating or drinking inappropriately before exercise can result in a full stomach or dehydration, the latter causing a lack of lubrication. Both can lead to a stitch. The best way of avoiding a stitch is to drink water or sports drinks, which empty from the stomach faster than concentrated drinks, such as cordials, soft drinks, or fruit juice. Drinking small quantities on a regular basis rather than consuming large volumes is also preferable.

The best way to get rid of a stitch? Stop exercising, bend forward, and tighten the abdominal muscles while taking deep breaths. A stitch is rarely a sign of a serious problem and usually passes a few minutes after the person with a stitch stops exercising.

❓ WHAT IS THE HISTORY OF THE PIZZA?

The pizza, in one form or another, has been around for thousands of years. Some claim it is based on pita bread, eaten in the Middle East. Some say that its origin is flatbreads, resembling the modern-day focaccia, which were eaten in ancient times around the Mediterranean. Archaeologists have uncovered structures resembling pizzerias in the remains of Pompeii, which was destroyed in AD 79 by the eruption of Mount Vesuvius. Evidence also suggests that the Greeks brought pizza to Italy in the AD first century. Flat baked breads covered in dressings were also said to be eaten in Rome in 300 BC.

The word *pizza*, meaning "pie," first appeared near Naples and Rome in AD 1000, and it is often accepted that Naples is the origin of the modern-day pizza, with the Neapolitan being the original pizza. The first modern-day pizzeria, which is still in existence, was opened in Naples by Raffaele Esposito in 1830. Pizza was considered food for the poor person, but to honor a visit by King Umberto I and Queen Margherita of Italy, Esposito created a special pizza resembling the Italian flag. The queen was impressed and the Margherita pizza was born.

The pizza was brought from Naples to the United States in 1897 by Gennaro Lombardi, who opened a general store in New York, which sold pizza. The pizzas became so popular that he opened the first American pizzeria in 1905. Called Lombardi's, the shop still operates today.

In the early 1900s in the United States, pizza was eaten predominantly by immigrant Italians. During World War II, American troops in Italy ate pizza extensively. When they returned, pizza became popular throughout the United States. Pizza shops began opening in the 1950s, and the trend spread quickly. Today, pizza is an international food.

WHAT MAKES DRUGS ADDICTIVE?

Drug addiction is the dependence on a substance to the point where the user feels that he or she must have the drug, regardless of consequences. Addiction varies from drug to drug. Compared with alcohol, it generally takes far less use of heroin to become addicted. Drug addiction also varies from person to person, and some people are genetically predisposed to it. The most common drug addictions are to alcohol, caffeine, and nicotine.

The addiction to drugs is either physical or psychological, or both. Physical dependency means the chemistry of the addict is altered so that he or she must have the drug or suffer symptoms of withdrawal. Without the drug, the addict might feel physically ill. Psychological dependency occurs when the person relies on the drug emotionally and craves it for feelings of reward. Without the drug the addict might feel stressed or fearful, so he or she keeps taking it to feel good.

Scientists believe that certain drugs (including cocaine and amphetamines) stimulate particular areas of the brain to release large amounts of dopamine, a chemical that occurs naturally in the brain and produces a feeling of euphoria. Other drugs (including alcohol) mimic endorphins, which have an effect that is similar to that of dopamine, and produce euphoria. After prolonged exposure to either type of drug, this feeling of euphoria can come to dominate the person's thoughts, and a physical or psychological dependency is the result.

Once the euphoria associated with a drug has passed, a protein is produced in the brain that inhibits the release of dopamine. This can leave the drug user depressed and unable to derive pleasure from previously enjoyable activities. This generally leads to the person taking the drug again to feel normal, often in larger doses because of the built-up level of tolerance. And so the cycle continues and the dependency increases.

HOW AND WHY DO CHAMELEON LIZARDS CHANGE COLOR?

The chameleon is a small lizard, found mainly in Africa and Madagascar (but also parts of Europe and Asia), that is famous for being able to change its color.

Most people believe that the chameleon changes color as a means of camouflage—it blends in with its surroundings. Not true. The lizard changes color depending on its physical or emotional disposition at the time. Chameleons change color in response to changes in light and temperature. The change of colors also depends on the mood of the lizard and plays a major role in communication with other chameleons. Their colors range from brown and green to red, blue, and yellow. Coincidentally, brown and green often match the chameleon's background, which leads people to think that camouflage is the reason for the change.

In cold conditions, a chameleon will turn a darker color to absorb more heat, and in hot and bright conditions, a chameleon will turn a lighter color to reflect the heat. To attract a mate, a male chameleon will exhibit his brightest and most impressive colors. If a rival male approaches, he will turn a bright color, such as red, indicating that he is a healthy specimen and ready to fight. If a chameleon is scared, it will often turn a dark color.

Chameleons are able to change colors because of their unusual genetics. Special cells lie in layers beneath their transparent skin. The upper layer contains red and yellow pigments, while the lower layer contains a colorless substance that reflects the blue part of light. Under these cells is a dark layer of melanin. This melanin influences how light or dark the reflected light is. Depending on the temperature, the brightness, or the chameleon's mood, hormones trigger the chameleon's brain to send a signal to activate particular cells. This message tells the cells to expand or contract, redistributing their colors and creating a different overall color for the lizard. For example, if the upper cells are yellow and the lower cells reflect the blue part of light, the colors mix and the chameleon turns green. The result of this unique chemistry is a lizard that can produce a wide variety of different colors to suit its circumstances.

WHY IS IT CALLED AN INDIAN SUMMER?

An Indian summer is a short period of warm and sunny weather just prior to winter. It usually occurs in autumn, sometime after the first frost of the year. The expression is also used to refer to a happy time that arrives near the end of something. This term has been used for more than two centuries, and its origin is unclear.

Many believe the phrase is based on American Indians raiding the European colonists. These raids generally occurred in the warm months, ceasing when it turned cold. If good weather returned in autumn, the raids would start again, and the period was said to be an Indian summer. There is a reference to this meaning in Joseph Doddridge's 1824 book *Notes on the Indian Wars in West Virginia*, but this theory is now considered inaccurate, because the term was first used in 1778, years after Indian raids had been commonplace.

Some say that Indian summer is the period when the early American colonists would harvest their crops, while others say that Indian summer is so named because it was more common in the territories of the American Indians (in the North and the West) than on the Eastern seaboard, which was largely populated by colonists. Another theory is that, like an Indian giver (an offensive term meaning a person who pretends to give a gift and then takes it back or expects a similar gift in return), an Indian summer is a false summer. Lending credence to this is the 1942 book *American Speech*: "'Tis but an Indian kind of summer after all, as false and fickle as they." Another proposed etymology is that the term originated with the practice of loading ships full of cargo when traveling across the Indian Ocean during a time of favorable weather conditions, or Indian summer. The name I.S.L. (an abbreviation for Indian Summer Line) was stamped on the hull of some ships.

Although more than one—or even many—of these theories about the origin of the term could be correct, the most credible is probably the one found in the 1778 book *Letters from an American Farmer* by Michel-Guillaume-Jean de Crevecoeur, a French-American farmer. The book refers to the winter being preceded by a short interval of smoke and mildness, called Indian summer. Other books discuss smoke during this period, and it is thought that this relates to the Indians either flushing out animals to hunt before the winter or burning the grassy areas in preparation for the following year's planting.

DID ROBINSON CRUSOE ACTUALLY EXIST?

In 1719, Daniel Defoe published the now-famous book *Robinson Crusoe*. The book is said to be based on the true story of Alexander Selkirk, a Scottish sailor born in 1676. Selkirk sailed on one of William Dampier's boats and, in 1704 while near the Juan Fernandez Islands, 400 miles off the coast of Chile, he had a dispute with the captain of the ship over the vessel's seaworthiness. Selkirk requested to be put ashore on one of the islands, where he would wait to be picked up by another passing ship. Selkirk lived alone on the uninhabited island for more than four years.

He took a musket and gunpowder, a knife, some tools, his clothing, and a Bible. At first, Selkirk remained on the beach and read the Bible while waiting for a passing rescue ship. None came. He slept in a cave before moving inland and building a permanent hut. Pestered at nighttime by rats, he domesticated feral cats to rid himself of the rodents. Freshwater was plentiful and there were goats on the island from earlier Spanish ships. He constantly kept a fire burning on a hillside in an attempt to attract passing ships.

Selkirk was industrious and made good use of what was available to him. He learned to make fire from rubbing wood together, fashioned clothes from goatskin, and tamed the wild goats. During his stay, two boats landed onshore, but because they were Spanish, Selkirk was forced to run and hide to avoid being killed. As the years passed, he began to revel in his solitude.

In 1709, Selkirk saw a boat, the *Duke*, bearing an English flag. The crew of the ship saw what they described as a "wildman." The pilot of the one of the longboats that came ashore was William Dampier, who vouched for Selkirk's story. Selkirk was rescued. As it turned out, his original decision to leave the ship saved his life. The ship had sunk near Peru, and its crew either drowned or were captured and imprisoned. Selkirk never readjusted to the civilized world, which he said "could not, with all its enjoyments, restore me to the tranquillity of my solitude." Within a few years, Selkirk returned to sea. He is thought to have died of yellow fever in 1721. One of the islands in the region where he was stranded bears his name, that of the real-life Robinson Crusoe.

? WHAT ARE THE HEALTH RISKS OF CELL PHONES?

Since the massive increase of cell phone use in recent years, health concerns have been raised, in particular whether they cause brain tumors. This has resulted in extensive research on both animals and people.

Cell phones use electromagnetic waves in the microwave range. Some of these waves can be absorbed into the human head. Microwaves are known to produce dielectric heating, in which living tissue is heated. With cell phone use, this

results in the temperature of the head increasing slightly. Some experts suggest that cell phone use may lead to brain tumors, although others say that the brain easily disposes of excess heat by regulating its blood circulation.

It is also thought that the levels of radiation emitted by cell phones damage the blood-brain barrier, which prevents harmful substances from entering the brain. Some studies have shown that the radiation causes the cells in blood vessels to shrink, allowing molecules to pass into the brain tissue. A 2004 study found evidence of DNA damage to cells, as well as gene and chromosome damage, and an increased rate of cell division (often associated with certain types of cancer). A more recent study from a Swedish team suggests that the radiation emitted causes damage to nerve fibers, potentially resulting in brain tumors. The study says that a person would probably have to use a cell phone for more than 10 years to be at risk.

Most of these studies have been carried out on animals, and it is unknown if the same effects would be seen in people. The majority of studies have found no substantive evidence that cell phones are harmful to human health. But no proof exists that they are safe either. Most experts agree that the current evidence is inconclusive. Nevertheless, the United Kingdom government advises that cell phone users exercise caution and keep call length to a minimum. In addition, those users younger than 16, whose nervous systems may still be developing, should take extra care to reduce their usage.

❓ WHAT IS THE ORIGIN OF HALLOWEEN?

Halloween falls on October 31 and is celebrated in much of the Western world. It usually involves children dressing up in costumes and knocking on doors in a ritual known as trick-or-treating. The theme of the night is ghosts, witches, and magic, with black cats, goblins, and candles in pumpkins being the prominent symbols.

Halloween's origin dates back to the pagan Celtic festival of Samhain. More than two thousand years ago, the Celts  celebrated their New Year on November 1. That day marked the end of the harvest and the beginning of the long winter, a time when death ran rife. The Celts believed that on the night before the New Year, the ghosts of the dead returned to Earth. The harvest festival began on October 31. Fires were lit and sacrifices of animals, crops, and even humans were offered to their gods. Those at the festival wore costumes and masks in an attempt to ward off evil spirits. An ember from the fire was given to each family on November 1 to take home for a new fire. This was thought to keep homes free from evil spirits throughout the winter.

When the Romans conquered the Celtic lands, they combined two of their festivals with the festival of Samhain. One was the festival of Pomona, which honored the goddess of fruit and trees, and the other was Feralia, a day in October when they honored the dead. By AD 800, Christianity had spread, and Pope Boniface IV made November 1 the day to honor saints and martyrs. It was All Saints' Day, also called All Hallows, from All Hallowed Souls. The night before was known as All Hallows Eve, which was eventually contracted to Halloween.

Trick-or-treating is thought to have originated with the European custom of "souling" in the AD 800s. On All Souls Day on November 2, beggars would walk from village to village, begging for bread with currants, known as soul cakes. In return for the cakes, the beggars would say prayers for the person's dead relatives, which were thought to assist the dead soul's passage to heaven.

Irish immigrants brought the custom of Halloween to America in the 1840s.

WHAT CAUSED THE GREAT DEPRESSION?

The Great Depression, which ran from 1929 until 1939, was a massive worldwide economic recession. It was the longest and most severe such contraction ever to hit the industrialized world and remains one of the most-studied economic events. Despite this, experts still disagree on its cause. Although the Wall Street stock market crash is often cited as the cause, most now agree it was actually caused by the inappropriate monetary policy adopted by the United States. The stock market crash was the first dramatic phase of the Depression, and it was brought about by the problems in the economy due to the prosperity of the 1920s. During that era, many people had plenty of money and abandoned traditional values of saving in order to spend lavishly on unessential items. But the wealth was spread out unevenly, and the rising incomes of the wealthy fueled a great increase in stock prices. Prices rose beyond the value of their companies, and in 1929 confidence that the prices would continue to rise faltered. Investors began selling stocks and prices rapidly plummeted.

The stock market crash affected banks and lending, leading to reduced levels of spending and a consequent lack of demand for production. Unemployment in the United States increased to 25 percent, while manufacturing decreased by one-third. The Depression quickly turned into a global crisis when the United States, the major creditor and financier of Europe following World War I, ceased its investment credits to Europe and sought the repayment of loans it had made to Germany. That country was then unable to pay the war reparations it owed to France and Britain, which were then unable to repay their loans to the United States. The world went into economic turmoil.

In an attempt to combat the crisis, various governments around the world employed restrictive policies and high tariffs and import duties. This resulted in a staggering drop in world trade. When Roosevelt was elected US president in 1932, he proposed what he called the New Deal, a policy of massive government spending intended to stimulate the economy. The British and French followed suit, but it wasn't until the United States entered World War II that public expenditure increased sufficiently and unemployment declined. The demand on American factories skyrocketed as they produced military supplies. After 10 years, the Depression finally ended.

 WHAT MAKES CHILI PEPPERS HOT?

The chili pepper is native to Mexico, where it has been used for thousands of years—some estimate since 7500 BC. They were also discovered in the Caribbean by Christopher Columbus and taken to Spain, from there they quickly spread to the rest of the world. Belonging to the same family as tomatoes and potatoes, chili peppers vary in shape, size, and texture, and their colors range from green to orange  to red. The heat of different chili peppers also varies, and the color of the chili is not necessarily indicative of its heat.

An alkaloid substance called capsaicin, along with four related chemicals, known as capsaicinoids, are responsible for the chili's distinctive hot, peppery taste. These chemicals are contained predominantly in the chili membrane to which the seeds are attached. Each capsaicinoid has a different effect on the mouth, generally stimulating the nerve receptors in the tongue and skin that sense heat and pain. If consumed to excess, capsaicin causes painful inflammation and even burns the skin.

The heat of chili peppers is measured in Scoville units (named after Wilbur Scoville, who developed the scale). The number of Scoville units indicates the amount of capsaicin present. Jalapeños generally average around 4,000 units, while the hottest chili, the naga jolokia from India, measures 855,000 units.

Scientists believe the reason chili peppers are hot is to repel mammals but not birds. Chili seeds pass straight through the digestive system of a bird, which helps disperse the seeds to grow new plants. However, the seeds do not pass through mammals. It is thought that chili peppers evolved to be hot so that mammals would not eat them, as that would hinder the spread of the seeds.

To mitigate the effects of eating a hot chili, some recommend ingesting salt, yogurt, mint leaves, cucumber, or milk. Drinking water often exacerbates the heat.

HOW DID THE SAYING "MIND YOUR P'S AND Q'S" ORIGINATE?

The expression "mind your p's and q's" means to be careful or prudent. It is said to have been first recorded in the 1600s. There are more than a few explanations as to its origin. Here are some of the theories about how this saying came to be:

- It is advice to typesetters not to confuse the letters when they face backward.
- *P* and *q* stand for "prime quality," which was written as *pee* and *kew* in the 1600s.
- It is a lecture to children not to confuse the two letters when learning the alphabet.
- It is a warning to sailors not to sully their navy pea jackets with their dirty pigtails, also known as queues.

- It is an instruction to dancers to perform the maneuvers pieds and queues correctly.
- It is a lesson to students studying both Latin and ancient Greek not to confuse *pente* and *quintus*.

But the most feasible explanation is that it means "to mind your pints and quarts." Years ago in taverns, innkeepers would keep a tally on a chalkboard behind the bar of the number of pints and quarts drunk by each person. Payment would be made by the patron at the end of the night or on the next payday. So that untrustworthy innkeepers did not add extra tally marks, patrons were wise to remain relatively sober to ensure they were not duped. Because sobriety tended to result in good behavior, the expression "mind your p's and q's" developed to mean just that.

Another credible explanation is that it is an abbreviation of "mind your pleases and thank-yous" (say "thank-yous" aloud and you'll hear the *q* sound). That said, the true origin of the expression is likely to remain a mystery.

IS THERE ANY SCIENCE TO HANDWRITING ANALYSIS?

Handwriting analysis, or graphology, is the study of handwriting and how it is connected to a person's behavior and personality. It has been in existence for thousands of years and is used mostly for employment profiling, marital compatibility, jury screening, psychological analysis, and even medical diagnosis. Forensic analysis to authenticate a document or determine whether a particular person wrote a document is not graphology. Graphology is based on the assumption that the brain and the central nervous system directly influence the movement of the hand. Graphologists believe that handwriting is the physical manifestation of the subconscious.

These are examples of how graphology claims to link handwriting and personality traits: letters slant to the left (has emotional control); letters slant to the right (is friendly and impulsive); the slants of letters are different (is versatile); small letters (is intelligent but has low self-esteem); large letters (is confident); massive letters (is theatrical and loud); narrow letters (is shy and self-disciplined); wide letters (is emotionally open); wide spaces between letters (prefers isolation); connecting letters (is cautious); perfect writing (is a good communicator); messy writing (is secretive); endings curve upward (is generous); and the *t* is crossed above the stem (is a daydreamer).

Graphologists once analyzed doodles made by Tony Blair at an economic forum. They concluded that the shapes of his words and drawings indicated he had a political death wish, the ability to come up with a fluent answer, and an inability to complete tasks. As it transpired, the doodles were in fact made by Bill Gates, the world's richest man, who certainly possessed an ability to complete tasks. Critics of graphology claim that graphologists rely on the content of what is written and that the lack of any scientific evidence makes it meaningless. The majority of studies conclude that it has no validity and that, in more than 70 percent of cases, graphologists cannot even determine the writer's gender.

Nevertheless, it was estimated in the 1980s that around 3,000 businesses in the US used graphology in screening potential employees, with suggestions that the number has grown considerably since that time.

 DO FISH EVER SLEEP?

People often wonder whether fish sleep. Scientists are not entirely certain of the answer.

Many fish exhibit resting behavior that resembles sleep. They enter an energy-saving state, which involves little or no movement. Apart from sharks, fish don't have any eyelids, so they are not capable of shutting their eyes, but nearly all fish do have long periods of inactivity. This period of inactivity is very different from their behavior during the rest of the day.

Perch, bass, and catfish often rest under logs at night, while parrot fish retire to a crevice and surround themselves with a mucus that they secrete. Tuna and herring tend to remain motionless for periods of the night, while other fish lean against rocks and move very little. Some dig holes in the  sand or mud to rest or simply float in a state of suspended animation. Some fish are dormant during the night, and others rest during the day.

Although fish appear to be asleep while they are resting, they are generally still alert to danger and are able to avoid predators.

Because of the difficulties inherent in studying the brain waves of fish, it is not known for sure whether they sleep in the same way that mammals do.

❓ WHY DO PEOPLE HAVE WISDOM TEETH?

Wisdom teeth are the third molars and usually come through after age 18. They get their name because they come later than other teeth, at an age when people are supposedly wise. These teeth are often angled awkwardly and need to be extracted because of their effect on other teeth.

It is thought that the human diet thousands of years ago is the reason for wisdom teeth. Before the invention of stone tools, coarse foods required more chewing power. Consequently, humans developed large and powerful jaws, which easily accommodated 35 teeth. Some experts also argue that teeth were more prone to decaying or being knocked out in ancient times, so the wisdom teeth would do the work of the lost teeth.

As technology developed, foods were softened by cooking and made into bite-size pieces by cutting. When large jaws were not necessary for survival, the energy used to grow and maintain them was used to fuel other parts of the body. Evolution reduced the size of the jaw, but the wisdom teeth remained. The incidence of tooth decay also declined, and the role of wisdom teeth was greatly reduced.

In modern times, the jaws of many people don't have the extra room for wisdom teeth. When these teeth cause problems, they are removed.

WHAT IS THE ORIGIN OF THE HANDSHAKE?

Handshaking is a common method of greeting across the world and is prevalent in both social and business settings.

Although most experts agree that handshaking is an ancient ritual, reported as far back as 2800 BC in Egypt, there is some argument as to its exact origin.

Some say the handshake evolved from the practice of Egyptian kings shaking the hand of a deity's statue to transfer the god's power to the king. The Egyptian hieroglyph for the word *give* was an outstretched hand.

Most historians now, however, agree that the handshake's origin lies in fighting between men. The right hand of a man was the one that traditionally carried a weapon, such as a sword or dagger. By presenting the right hand openly, it showed that the man was not carrying a weapon and that he meant no harm to the other man.

Because women did not usually carry weapons, they did not partake in handshaking. The custom has developed in modern times, particularly as a result of the entry of women

into business, and handshaking is now common for both sexes. As in ancient times, the modern handshake is a symbol of peace and acceptance, along with equality and openness.

? WHAT IS STOCKHOLM SYNDROME?

Stockholm syndrome describes the psychological response of hostages who develop feelings of sympathy for their captors. It is named after a 1973 hostage incident in Stockholm, Sweden, in which bank robbers held bank employees for six days. The hostages became emotionally attached to the robbers, so much so that some resisted rescue attempts. After the incident was over, some of the hostages refused to testify against their captors.

The syndrome is thought to exist when a hostage cannot escape and is threatened with death or violence but shown the occasional act of kindness, which the hostage interprets as magnanimous. As a subconscious survival strategy, a hostage might identify with the captor in order to keep the captor happy. After a few days, this can lead to the hostage actually sympathizing with the captor. Psychologists point out that the syndrome arises only in extreme situations. In such an instance, rational thinking might be impossible.

There are many examples of people with this syndrome, including Patty Hearst. After she was taken hostage, she joined her captors in a bank robbery. The main symptom of the syndrome is the hostage's inexplicable loyalty to a person in a more powerful position even though that person puts the hostage in danger. The syndrome is thought to account for the victims of domestic abuse and child abuse who love and identify with their abusers. Military commanders exploit a mild form of the syndrome by adopting abusive training techniques in order to build loyalty and hold the unit together. It has also been seen in prisoners of war and in those held in concentration camps.

Evolutionary psychologists suggest that the syndrome stems from the tendency of babies to emotionally attach to a parent to increase the probability of that parent ensuring that the baby survives.

Despite numerous examples of the syndrome, the FBI estimates that 92 percent of hostage victims exhibit no sign of Stockholm syndrome.

 ## HOW DOES TEAR GAS WORK?

Tear gas is any chemical agent used to cause temporary pain to the eyes or respiratory system. It is often used in grenade form by police or the military as a means of riot control. Tear gas temporarily incapacitates a person by irritating the eyes, causing tears to flow and rendering the victim unable to open the eyes. It can also induce vomiting.

Used in warfare since ancient times, tear gas is a lacrimatory (from the Latin word meaning "a tear") substance, producing tears because of one or more chemical compounds, abbreviated as CS, CN, and CR. CS and CR irritate the mucous membranes in the eyes, nose, and mouth. These compounds are chosen for their ability to produce tears, while still being of a low toxicity. CS (or o-chlorobenzylidene-malononitrile) is now the most widely used tear gas.

CS is favored because it can be rapidly neutralized by water. CS actually decomposes in water, whereas CN and CR are only removed by it.

While considered nonlethal, CS tear gas generally causes increased problems for those with asthma, bronchitis, liver disease, or kidney disease. Also, the very young and very old might be more sensitive to it.

In addition to producing tears, tear gas can burn and irritate the skin. Its effects usually occur within seconds and are reduced within about 30 minutes. Dogs and horses are much less sensitive to tear gas, allowing them to work in riots when this chemical agent is employed.

WHY DID DINOSAURS BECOME EXTINCT?

The dinosaurs became extinct about 65 million years ago, having existed for more than 165 million years. Their time on Earth amounts to around 75 percent of the history of the planet, making their extensive dominance the most successful of nearly any life-form. The reason such a flourishing group went extinct has been the subject of much research, and until recently was one of the most perplexing riddles facing paleontologists.

Despite years of research, it is only since 1980 that scientists have had some firm evidence about the cause of the demise of the dinosaurs. A theory was proposed by geologist Walter Alvarez, whose team discovered fossilized sedimentary layers across the world from the end of the Cretaceous period and the start of the Tertiary period, 65 million years ago (known as the Cretaceous-Tertiary boundary). The fossils contain a high concentration of iridium, an element that is rare on Earth but common in objects such as asteroids and comets. Alvarez concluded that a 10-kilometer-wide asteroid collided with Earth and led to the death of the dinosaurs. It is known as the KT extinction event (K being an abbreviation of Cretaceous). Evidence has now been found that such an asteroid did slam into Yucatán.

A collision of that magnitude would have been millions of times more powerful than any nuclear weapon and would have resulted in enormous hurricanes and a worldwide firestorm. Dust from extensive storms would have filled the atmosphere, blocking sunlight for years, producing acid rain, and dramatically reducing world temperatures, thus wiping out the dinosaurs.

Although most scientists agree that the KT event led to the extinction of the dinosaurs, it is unknown whether they died off rapidly. The majority of experts favor this view. But another theory is that increased volcanic activity across the world made oxygen decrease and temperatures drop, killing off the dinosaurs gradually. Some say that the dinosaurs were killed by disease as they migrated throughout the world, but most experts think that this is unlikely.

❓ WHAT IS HOUSEHOLD DUST?

Dust is the collective name for tiny solid particles that occur in the atmosphere. It comprises pieces of soil made airborne by the wind and minute specks of various forms of pollution.

Household dust is a common form of dust and is present in every home. It consists of dust from the atmosphere, as well as mold, animal dander, food particles, insect waste, small fibers from clothing and bedding, and the sloughed-off skin cells of the members of the household.

Dust mites are also part of dust. These microscopic, insectlike creatures are found in the warmth and humidity of carpets and bedding. They feed on the skin cells in the dust, and their excrement then also forms part of the dust.

It is this dust mite excrement that is highly allergenic and often causes people to sneeze and cough, even after the dust mite that produced it has died. The excrement is so small that it can be easily dislodged and made airborne by walking on it. Studies in the United Kingdom show that 90 percent of those with allergic asthma are allergic to dust mites.

Female dust mites can lay up to 50 eggs, producing a new generation every three weeks. It is thought that virtually no amount of vacuuming or cleaning can completely eradicate dust mites.

IS TIME TRAVEL POSSIBLE?

The idea of time travel fascinates humanity. H. G. Wells's novel *The Time Machine* dealt with the concept in 1895, and science fiction writers have been exploring it ever since. Time travel is a fanciful notion, but as science has developed, it has been viewed as increasingly possible. The various theories about how to time travel, which feature wormholes, parallel universes, and spinning cylinders, involve complex, inconclusive mathematical principles.

It is generally accepted that it is impossible to travel back in time to before an event and affect the event that has already transpired. To do this would mean recreating every aspect of the universe, including the position of every planet and star, and the exact motion of every molecule at the time. It is impossible. Similarly, to travel into the future and "suspend animation," so that time passes but the traveler's body is unaffected, is also impossible. There is no way to do this—but some theorists suggest it might be possible.

The area of time travel that is most frequently debated, and that some scientists now consider a possibility, is going back in time and viewing (although not participating in) the past. Einstein's theories of relativity show how time changes with motion and suggest that, compared with a stationary observer, time appears to pass more slowly for bodies that are moving at a faster speed. Time is not always a constant, and by increasing speed, the passage of time can be altered.

When we look at something, we see the light beams emitted at the time that the light beams are sent. If we are able to travel faster than the speed of light, we can overtake the light and see it actually being sent. An example of this is the light given off by the stars. What we see are the light beams given off years ago, so if we could travel faster than them, we could see them being emitted and see the event that they are emitting. In other words, we view a past event by overtaking the light beams that carried that event. Although this time travel is possible in theory, it would mean traveling faster than 186,000 miles per second. This is not possible at present, and there is no experimental evidence to indicate that it ever will be possible. It is all theory.

WHY DO PEOPLE'S FEET SWELL DURING AIRPLANE TRAVEL?

Swelling (or edema) of the feet is a common complaint of travelers on long flights.

Many blame the decreased atmospheric pressure at a high altitude. However, the usual cause of the swelling is inactivity. This can occur on the ground as well.

When a flier is seated for hours on a plane, his or her posture causes constriction in many blood vessels. This results in the heart having to work harder to pump blood. To lighten the burden, excess fluids flow to the body's extremities, causing the feet to swell. Because of the low position of the legs, gravity causes blood to pool in the feet, increasing the swelling. Increased pressure in the veins because of the position of the legs also causes fluids to leave the blood and move into the tissues of the feet.

The best way to reduce this swelling is to move the feet or walk around. Walking uses muscles throughout the body, which compresses veins and forces blood back to the heart. Elevating the feet can also alleviate symptoms. Drinking plenty of fluids to avoid dehydration is also helpful.

Although swelling of the feet generally lessens shortly after a flight, prolonged swelling through a lack of movement can result in a blood clot in the leg. This is known as deep vein thrombosis (or DVT) and requires prompt medical attention.

WHAT IS THE ORIGIN OF THE TERM "HONEYMOON"?

It is commonly thought that the word *honeymoon* comes from a supposed Babylonian custom of drinking mead, or honey beer.

It is said that the father of the bride would provide the groom with honey beer for the first lunar month of the marriage. The drink was said to increase fertility and virility. So *honey* from the beer and *moon* from the lunar month made the complete word, and the first month of a marriage became the honeymoon.

It is now thought that the mead-drinking theory is a myth. The first written reference to the word *honeymoon* was in 1552 by Richard Huloet, well after the days of Babylon. Samuel Johnson also referred to it in the 1600s.

Both Huloet and Johnson define *honeymoon* as the first month after marriage, when things are sweet like honey. It is thought that *moon* relates to the lunar month. Samuel Johnson also proposed another explanation: Like the moon, the sweetness of the marriage quickly wanes.

WHAT CAUSES "THE SHAKES" AFTER DRINKING A LOT OF ALCOHOL?

The day after drinking large quantities of alcohol, the drinker's hands might shake and tremble, making it difficult to perform a simple task, such as turning the s of a newspaper.

These shakes are a mild form of delirium tremens, or the DTs, a condition associated with withdrawal from a sustained instance or period of heavy drinking.

The symptoms of an acute case of the DTs include severe tremors (mainly of the hands), vivid hallucinations, anxiety, and insomnia. Blood pressure can also increase dramatically and unpredictably, as can the rate of breathing. These symptoms can lead to a heart attack. Nausea and vomiting are also often symptoms. The tremors usually begin within five to ten hours after the last drink and continue for one to two days.

The DTs are caused by the effect of alcohol on the brain receptors for the inhibitory neurotransmitter gamma-aminobutyric acid (GABA). When drinking stops, there are not as many receptors to which GABA can attach. Because GABA normally inhibits action, fewer receptors mean that activation is unhindered. Put simply, with prolonged alcohol abuse, the brain becomes accustomed to the depressing effect of alcohol and produces naturally stimulating chemicals to compensate. Once the alcohol is removed, the chemicals remain, leading to the brain being overstimulated. Tremors and hallucinations are the result.

Alcohol withdrawal is common, with many drinkers experiencing a mild case of the shakes. However, the DTs occur in only 5 percent of those going through alcohol withdrawal.

The DTs are a very serious condition, killing about one in twenty sufferers. To help prevent the DTs, heavy drinkers can take vitamins and minerals.

HOW DO ANIMALS HIBERNATE?

Hibernation allows certain animals to conserve energy and sleep through the winter months. Most animals choose a secluded place to hibernate, such as a cave or burrow. Some animals awaken periodically and eat food they have stored, while others sleep for a whole season. The reason animals hibernate is to survive the cold months and also because food is difficult to find in the winter.

During hibernation, the metabolism of an animal is reduced to a very low level, along with the breathing rate and heart rate. Also, the body temperature is reduced (to a level that can match the ambient temperature). During this time, the animal gradually uses up fat stores for energy. When asleep, an animal moves and has an active brain, whereas with true hibernation the animal appears dead and can even be touched without being aware of it.

To prepare for hibernation, most animals eat a lot of food so that they can store fat deposits to help them survive the winter. The animals use these fat stores and do not lose any muscle bulk. This means they come out of hibernation with the strength they need to hunt.

Both land and aquatic animals hibernate, including mice, bats, frogs, snakes, and squirrels. Cold-blooded animals hibernate when cold weather causes their body temperatures to drop. Bears are popularly depicted as hibernating in winter, but they are not true hibernators. At this time of year, the heart rate of a bear slows, but the body temperature remains fairly constant, and the bear can be easily roused.

By giving them hydrogen sulphide, scientists have artificially induced hibernation in mice. This raises the possibility of inducing hibernation in other animals, including humans.

WHAT IS TRUTH SERUM AND DOES IT WORK?

Truth serum is a drug used to try to obtain accurate answers from a person who is being questioned. It is normally used by police or military interrogators. Its existence has been popularized by motion pictures, in particular, the James Bond film *Octopussy*, Arnold Schwarzenegger's *True Lies*, and more recently *Kill Bill*.

A number of sedatives have been used as truth serums, but the most common is sodium thiopental, known as Sodium Pentothal. This yellow crystal can be dissolved in alcohol or water.

Sodium Pentothal interferes with the part of the brain that controls judgment. Patients typically lose their normal inhibitions and become very communicative. The drug slows the central nervous system, reducing the heart rate and blood pressure. It minimizes stress and excitement and makes patients more relaxed and open to suggestion. This might make patients more likely to tell the truth.

But although patients' inhibitions are lowered, they do not lose self-control and so are still able to lie, fantasize, or be manipulated into telling lies.

Truth serums were tested in the United States in the 1950s, and although they can be effective facilitators of questioning, they were found not to be the magical drug that had been claimed. In fact, studies show that information obtained through truth serums is often unreliable, and although some assert that government agencies possess more powerful and successful truth drugs, anesthetics experts doubt this claim.

A number of US court decisions have disallowed evidence obtained using truth serum, finding such testimony unreliable.

❓ WHY DON'T BIRDS FALL OFF BRANCHES WHEN ASLEEP?

People often wonder why birds don't fall from a perch when they go to sleep.

Birds' feet prevent them from falling. Their feet are similar to our hands, generally with three toes fanned forward and one pointing to the rear.

Many birds' feet can do an array of tasks, including walking, hopping, and holding on to objects. The sharp claws and long toes of birds allow them to balance in a multitude of positions and cling to rough surfaces.

When a bird lands on a branch, its opposing toes wrap around the branch tightly. The muscles in the bird's legs contain long tendons, and when the bird clasps a branch, the tendons tighten and the toes lock. This involuntary reflex fastens the bird to the branch. The more the bird bends its legs, the greater the pull on the tendons and the firmer the grip on the branch. Once the feet are locked on to the branch, the bird can safely sleep without risking falling off.

To release its grasp, the bird stands up and straightens its legs. This releases the tendons. It actually takes less effort for a bird to stay on a branch than to let go.

❓ WHY IS THE BERMUDA TRIANGLE SUCH A FEARED BOATING AREA?

The Bermuda Triangle is a 1.5-million–square–mile area of ocean situated between Bermuda, Puerto Rico, and the tip of Florida. It is famous because of the supposedly inordinate number of unexplained boat and plane disappearances in the region. The suspicious circumstances under which vessels have disappeared have led some to believe that the Bermuda Triangle, also known as the Devil's Triangle, possesses paranormal forces that contravene the laws of physics.

The Bermuda Triangle found fame in the 1950s when a number of "mysterious disappearances" were reported. It was then highly publicized in the 1974 book *The Bermuda Triangle*, which described several inexplicable events, including the 1945 loss of a squadron of five navy aircraft, known as Flight 19. To add to the mysticism, the US Navy ascribed the loss to unknown causes. The book prompted many theories, both natural and supernatural.

Some experts attribute the phenomenon to the amount of methane hydrates in the area's continental shelves. It is said that methane eruptions are capable of producing enormous bubbles that can sink ships. Some say the amount of gas in the water also renders the water buoyantless, causing ships to sink without warning. The methane gas in the atmosphere is also said to make the air less dense, causing planes to lose lift and crash. Less-dense air also interrupts the altimeters on planes, giving the impression that the plane is climbing, which can result in the plane diving and crashing. Others say that freak waves in the area can cause ships to sink, and the high electromagnetic activity there can cause problems with electronic equipment. Unpredictable weather patterns and the turbulent Gulf Stream waters are also cited as explanations.

The US Coast Guard, however, does not recognize the Bermuda Triangle as an exceptional area, remarking that the incidence of lost ships and planes is no greater there than in any other heavily traversed area. It chalks up the disappearances to human error, including a lack of local knowledge and poor seamanship. Major insurance companies do not charge greater insurance premiums for travel in the area.

WHY DO FINGERS WRINKLE IN WATER?

A bather who is in the water for a long time will note that his or her fingers and toes turn wrinkly.

The human skin is covered with a special oil called sebum. It is not visible to the naked eye but is produced by the epidermis, the outermost layer of skin. Sebum is the reason we leave oily fingerprints on the objects we touch. It moistens, lubricates, and protects the skin. It also acts to waterproof the skin. Sebum is the reason that water runs off the skin instead of soaking in.

After a long time in the water, the layer of sebum gets washed away, allowing the water to penetrate the skin. This leaves the skin waterlogged, causing it to swell in some places but not others. This gives the skin its wrinkly appearance. The condition is most noticeable on the feet and hands, where the skin is thickest.

After the bather leaves the water, the absorbed water quickly evaporates, and the wrinkles on the fingers disappear. The skin returns to normal and develops a new coating of protective sebum.

DID SANTA CLAUS REALLY EXIST?

Santa Claus (known by different names in different places) is a mythical Christmas character popular in Western culture. Also known as Father Christmas, he is said to live at the North Pole, where he and his elves make presents, which he delivers on Christmas Eve by traveling the world on a flying sleigh pulled by reindeer. Portrayed as a portly, white-bearded old man in a red suit, he gains entry to houses by sliding down the chimney.

Santa Claus is thought to be based on a real-life man, Saint Nicholas of Myra, an AD fourth-century bishop in a province of Byzantium, which today is in

Turkey. A religious man, he was famous for his generosity, particularly to the poor, and reportedly gave dowries of gold to three daughters of a Christian man to prevent them from being forced into prostitution.

Although there is no written evidence that the real Santa Claus existed, we do know from folklore that a boy named Nicholas was born around AD 255 to a wealthy family. His parents are said to have died when he was young, and he traveled extensively throughout Egypt and Palestine, using his wealth to help the poor. After being appointed a bishop, he was imprisoned by the Roman emperor Diocletian, who persecuted Christians, but was later released by another Roman emperor, Constantine the Great. When he died, Nicholas was buried in his church at Myra and was later declared a saint. During the Middle Ages, his legend as a bringer of gifts became famous throughout Europe, and many churches were named after him.

The Dutch brought the legend of Saint Nicholas to the United States, calling him Sinterklaas. The name Sinterklaas was later Americanized to Santa Claus.

HOW DID CHOPSTICKS ORIGINATE?

Chopsticks are the traditional eating utensils of most of Asia. They are a pair of sticks, equal in length, that are held in one hand and used to pick up food. They can be made of wood, bamboo, bone, ivory, metal, or plastic. Some say that silver chopsticks were used by Chinese royalty to detect poison in the food. Poison would react with the silver, turning it black.

Chopsticks is from the pidgin English word *chop*, meaning "quick." The Mandarin word for *chopsticks* is *kuàizi*, which means "the bamboo objects for eating quickly."

It is thought that chopsticks were developed in China around five thousand years ago. Food was cooked in large pots, and people would break off tree twigs and sticks to retrieve it from the pot. As the population of China grew rapidly, resources became scarce and food was cut into small pieces so that it  would cook faster and less fuel would be consumed. These small cuts of food eliminated the need for knives, and chopsticks came to be used for the whole meal. Confucius also perpetuated the use of chopsticks by dissuading people from having knives at the table. He was a vegetarian and associated knives with slaughterhouses.

By AD 500, chopsticks had spread to Korea, Vietnam, and Japan. Originally used in Japan only for religious ceremonies, they quickly became popular and widespread.

Many Asians believe that the use of chopsticks improves the memory, learning skills, and dexterity. Some superstitions surround chopsticks. It is thought that a person eating with an uneven pair of chopsticks will miss the next boat, plane, or train. Dropping chopsticks is considered a sign of bad luck to come.

WHAT IS EXORCISM AND IS IT SUCCESSFUL?

Exorcism is the process of removing evil spirits that "possess" a person from that person's body. Symptoms of being possessed by an evil spirit are the ability to speak a foreign language without knowledge of that language, making blasphemous comments, having an aversion to God, and having seemingly supernatural powers or strength. Exorcism received wide publicity with the famous 1973 horror movie *The Exorcist*, which was based on an actual Catholic exorcism.

Exorcists are usually priests who employ an array of methods, such as prayers, rituals, and gestures, to drive the evil from the person. The practice, which is considered dangerous, is entrusted only to senior religious people.

Exorcists have been practicing since ancient times. The New Testament speaks of exorcisms performed by Jesus, and these accounts have helped keep the custom part of Christianity. Pope John Paul II performed three exorcisms while pope and reinforced the importance of the practice as late as 2000. Exorcism has also been present in Islam since its inception (the Koran refers to it). According to Islam, evil spirits made from fire, known as Jinn, can possess people. In the Hindu religion, exorcisms are elaborate and involve hitting the person with neem leaves.

Despite exorcism being common to many religions, because of the advances of modern-day medicine, exorcisms are generally performed only after consultation with medical professionals to ensure that the person is actually "possessed," not mentally ill. Because of these advances in medicine, many experts place no credence in exorcism.

HOW IS A SAFE CRACKED?

The idea of safecracking has been popularized by movies such as *Ocean's Eleven, The Italian Job*, and *The Score*, in which people use listening devices to determine the code of rotary combination locks. In reality, safecracking is far more intricate than this cinematic depiction.

Different methods of safecracking are used, depending on the type of safe. The simplest way to crack a safe is to guess the code. Manufacturers have standard combinations for safes, which purchasers are supposed to change. But many purchasers fail to do this, so the original combination remains. Drilling is another common method. Holes are drilled to see the internal mechanics of the lock  or to bypass the lock and gain access to the safe. Hardplate steel is often used in safes to ensure against this, as is the insertion of a glass plate, which, when broken, prompts additional bolts to lock to protect the safe. Removing the outer shell of a safe ("peeling"), using explosives, and using blowtorches to burn through a safe are other methods.

A common method is breaking the code of a rotary combination safe by using sound or feel, as seen in movies.

This is safecracking in its purest form and requires patience. The safecracker first determines the contact points on the lock. Where the levers in the lock contact each other, there is a small click. The safecracker listens or feels for this click, and then sees what number on the dial corresponds with the click. Because a combination can contain between one and eight numbers, each with a corresponding wheel, the safecracker must then determine how many wheels there are. The safecracker turns the dial, listening for clicks. Each click represents a wheel. As each click is heard, the dial is stopped and the wheel is "parked." Each wheel is picked, one at a time, until none remain. The results of each click and the corresponding numbers are then graphed. This represents the range of numbers that hold the combination but not their order. The numbers are then dialed in all possible variations until the safe opens. Needless to say, this process can be very time consuming.

WHAT IS THE HISTORY OF BULLFIGHTING?

Bullfighting, a popular blood sport, is performed in some countries around the world but mostly in Spain, where it was born.

The sport has ancient origins. The Bible mentions that sacrifices of bulls will not take away sins (Hebrews 10:4). And bullfighting was part of the religious ceremonies of tribes who lived in prehistoric Spain. It is also linked to ancient Rome, where people were pitted against bulls as a warm-up for gladiatorial events. This probably originated from the Mediterranean practice of sacrificing bulls.

Sports involving bulls were probably brought to Spain by the Moors in the AD eleventh century. The bull was originally fought from horseback in Spain. In 1726, Francisco Romero began fighting on foot. Ronda, Spain, is said to boast the first bullring, which opened in 1785. Juan Belmonte is credited with inventing the modern-day style of Spanish bullfighting, using daring and dangerous maneuvers in which he kept his body very close to the bull as it passed.

Bullfighting spread to Latin America before arriving in France in the 1800s. It received American recognition in the 1920s and '30s, owing to Ernest Hemingway's novel *The Sun Also Rises* and his detailed commentary on bullfighting in *Death in the Afternoon*.

Bullfighting is a controversial sport, criticized heavily by animal rights activists, who see it as a cruel and wasteful

death. Bullfighting aficionados claim that the bulls are bred for fighting and live far better lives than cattle that are used for meat. It has been banned in Morocco and Brazil but remains extremely popular in Spain.

❓ CAN THE FULL MOON AFFECT HUMAN BEHAVIOR?

Since the Middle Ages, it has been said that the full moon has bizarre effects on human behavior. It is commonly thought to bring out the worst in people, increasing crime and suicide rates, making people more aggressive, and making accidents more prevalent. The influence of the full moon is known as the lunar effect. Even the word *lunacy* (meaning "insanity") is derived from the Latin word *lunar*, meaning "of or relating to the moon." In the 1800s, a murderer could rely on the defense of lunacy if the crime was committed during a full moon.

Even today, many people take the notion of a lunar effect seriously. Some studies in the United Kingdom show that car accidents rise by up to 50 percent during a full moon. A University of Miami psychologist, Arnold Lieber, also studied the homicide rate for 15 years. He found an increased rate corresponded with the full moon throughout that time. He then repeated the experiment using data from Cleveland, Ohio, and the same result was found.

One proposed reason for the lunar effect is the fact that a woman's menstrual cycle is, on average, the same length as the 28-day cycle of the moon. Another is the effect of the moon on the water contained in our bodies. Like the surface of Earth, the human body is 80 percent water. Some theorize that people experience some sort of biological tide, similar to the tides of the ocean. Skeptics counter this argument by pointing out that, unlike the ocean, the amount of water in the body is far too small to have tides. Even land-locked lakes do not experience tides. In any event, the tides in oceans occur twice a day, not once a month, and the tidal force of the moon depends on the moon's distance from Earth and not on its phase. They also say that the full moons in the car accident studies fell during weekends, when the traffic volume was higher. They further claim that the statistical methods used for the homicide rate data are dubious, and when calculated using other methods, the lunar effect is nonexistent. The many studies done by skeptics show no correlation between the moon and human behavior. These skeptics say that the perceived lunar effect is folklore that people want to believe. Further, skeptics assert that because of media hype about the lunar effect, people often assume a causal connection between strange incidents and the full moon.

HOW AND WHEN DID RUSSIAN ROULETTE ORIGINATE?

Russian roulette is a perverse game in which one bullet is placed in a revolver, the cylinder is spun around and then closed, and, while the gun is aimed at the player's own head, the player pulls the trigger. This game of chance can have dire consequences. With a six-bullet-capacity cylinder, there is about a 17 percent chance that the person will be killed.

There are several theories as to the origin of this perilous pastime. One theory is that it began in Russia in the 1800s—prisoners were forced to play the game while guards bet on the outcome. Another theory is that desperate or suicidal officers in the Russian army played it in front of other men. Russian officers had a penchant for violence, and corroborating this theory is the first known usage of the term. It is in the short story "Russian Roulette" by Georges Surdez that was published in a 1937 edition of *Collier's* magazine, in

which he describes the game and refers to Tsarist troops in Romania engaging in it during World War I.

Although it is not clear whether the game was ever played in the Russian army, the cylinder of the revolver issued in the late 1800s and early 1900s to Russian army personnel was not capable of being spun. This means that the standard Russian gun of the time was unsuitable for the game.

The 1978 movie *The Deer Hunter* showed Russian roulette being played by soldiers in the Vietnam War, but there is little other evidence to suggest this conflict as the origin of the pastime. However, it is thought that the vivid scenes in the movie sparked an interest in the game, resulting in a spate of deaths.

The exact origin of the game is unlikely to ever be known.

WHY ARE BLACK CATS CONSIDERED UNLUCKY?

Historically, black cats have been accused of bringing bad luck. Their ability to lurk in the shadows and remain unseen has made them seem untrustworthy. Even today, it is a well-known superstition.

The earliest association of black cats with evil comes from ancient Hebrew and Babylonian mythology. They were compared with serpents coiled on a hearth. Black cats were also symbolically associated with witchcraft.

Lore held that black cats were kept by witches as pets and used in magical rituals. In fact, in early witch trials, ownership of a black cat was considered evidence of a Satanic affiliation, resulting in both the witch and the cat being burned alive.

Throughout many parts of Europe in the Middle Ages, the black cat was considered bad luck. The Germans believed that if a black cat jumped on the bed of a sick person, that person was likely to die, while the Normans thought that if a black cat crossed a person's path in the moonlight, that person would die in an epidemic. The Chinese believed a black cat meant that sickness and poverty were approaching. In Finland, black cats were said to carry the souls of the dead to the next world.

This sentiment has continued until the modern day, although in some parts of Europe, cats of any color are thought to bring good fortune, and if a cat walks into your house it is considered a blessing.

WHAT CAUSES POSTNATAL DEPRESSION?

It is estimated that up to 80 percent of women experience a mild case of depression after having a child, and approximately 10 percent develop postnatal depression, a more serious condition. Also known as postpartum depression, symptoms can range from anger to anxiety to depression to guilt.

The cause of postnatal depression is not clear. Many theories exist, including one or more factors such as low self-esteem, prenatal anxiety, a poor marital relationship, being a single parent, an unplanned or unwanted pregnancy, a history of previous depression, or low socioeconomic status.

Although hormonal changes are often cited as the reason for postnatal depression, there is little evidence to support this, and in fact, fathers are also known to suffer the condition.

Some assert that postnatal depression is no more common than depression from other causes, while many claim it is due to a new mother's feelings of isolation, worry, and responsibility, especially in cases where there is a lack of social support.

Evolutionists believe that postnatal depression is rooted in the fact that in ancient times a mother reduced her investment in a child when the costs outweighed the benefits. For example, if times were hard and the mother had inadequate social support, she might not have been able to raise the child without damaging her own health or the health of her other children. This neglect was then likely to cause feelings of guilt.

Long-term depression can become a real problem for both mother and baby. It can result in the mother becoming exhausted, being unable to cope with her situation, and not providing adequate care for the baby. In serious cases, medication and therapy are recommended.

HOW IS MONEY COUNTERFEITED?

Money has been counterfeited ever since it was invented. In fact, according to the United States Department of Treasury, an estimated 70 million counterfeit dollars are in circulation.

Traditionally, counterfeiting used large, expensive printing presses and metal plates. This process involved making negatives of banknotes with a camera, cleaning the negatives and touching them up, and then burning them onto presensitized aluminum plates. Each plate showed the exact details of the note, which was then run through an offset printing press so that the note had a front and a back. Fake serial numbers were carefully added to the notes. The notes were then cut to size. Because the replicated notes were white, they then needed to be dyed the color of the real notes—green food dye was often used for US currency.

Another popular method was to use real banknotes of small denominations and bleach out the distinguishing markings of the denomination. The markings of higher denominated notes were then added in using the preceding method.

Since the advances in computer technology of the past two decades, money can be counterfeited more simply, using a computer, a scanner, and a color inkjet printer. The note is put on the scanner, which is set at its highest resolution. Using a high-quality printer to avoid losing any of the note's detail, the note is then printed (both back and front), neatly aligned, and cut to size.

The type of paper used is also important to give it a feel similar to that of money. Rag paper, which contains cotton and linen fibers, is the best.

Governments employ anticounterfeiting measures, such as embedding plastic or metal security strips in the notes, adding holograms or watermarks to the notes, making the notes an array of different colors, or using color-shifting ink.

❓ HOW HARMFUL IS PASSIVE SMOKING?

Passive smoking (also known as secondhand smoking or environmental tobacco smoking) is a controversial topic and the subject of many studies. It involves people who don't smoke inhaling the cigarette smoke of people who do.

Many experts believe that passive smokers are at risk of developing most of the problems that actual smokers develop. Studies published in prominent medical journals have found many detrimental effects of passive smoking. The *Journal of the American Medical Association* con- cluded that up to 40,000  deaths in the United States during the 1980s were caused by passive smoking. Other studies have found that passive smoking increases the likelihood of heart disease by up to 60 percent. Passive smoking appears to be particularly dangerous for children, contributing to sudden infant death syndrome and several respiratory diseases.

A 1997 study published in the *British Medical Journal* found a 24 percent greater incidence of lung cancer in nonsmokers who lived with smokers. In addition, the study found that tobacco-specific carcinogens were found in the blood of these passive smokers, indicating the significant risks involved.

The Tobacco Manufacturers' Association tries to discredit the various studies by pointing out that the results of the studies differ. Some studies have found only a weak connection between diseases and passive smoking, which the tobacco companies have seized on as evidence that passive smoking is not harmful.

Most experts, however, now agree that passive smoking is harmful. In light of the body of evidence, and the fact that smokers have a choice to smoke but passive smokers don't, many governments worldwide have banned smoking in the workplace and in quite a few public areas, including restaurants.

WHAT IS THE HISTORY OF THE SWASTIKA?

The swastika symbol is a cross with each of its arms bent at right angles. Although commonly associated with Nazi Germany, it actually has been in existence for thousands of years. The word *swastika* derives from a Sanskrit word *svastika*, meaning "any lucky or auspicious object."

The swastika has been found on pottery from as far back as 5000 BC, as well as on pottery found at the Sintashta archaeological site in Russia, dating from 2000 BC.

The symbol was also adopted by the Native Americans, as well as the Hittites, Celts, and ancient Greeks. It is considered a sacred symbol in Hinduism, Buddhism, and Jainism. Its significance varies but it often represents either the sun or luck. Today, it is still used in religious ceremonies in India and is common throughout the world, still signifying good luck.

Some archaeologists theorize that the use of the symbol is widespread because the swastika is a simple symbol, easily drawn on pottery. Others say that its use spread through cultural diffusion.

Since the formation of the Nazi Party in Germany prior to World War II, the swastika has had negative connotations. The Nazis used it as a symbol of the Aryan master race. Because the Nazis committed atrocities, many still associate the swastika solely with Nazis and are not aware of its historical roots and spiritual meaning. Even today, the symbol is used by neo-Nazis and other extremist groups.

WHAT IS THE ORIGIN OF "HIS NAME IS MUD"?

The expression "his name is mud" applies to someone who is despised for something he has done.

The common belief is that the saying derives from Samuel Mudd, MD. When John Wilkes Booth assassinated the US president Abraham Lincoln in 1865, Booth broke an ankle while escaping. Dr. Mudd treated Booth's broken ankle, was convicted of being involved in a conspiracy, and was sentenced to prison. The expression "his name is mud" referred to Dr. Mudd's act of treachery.

But in fact, the expression first appeared in writing in 1820, well before the Lincoln assassination. It is thought to pertain to the eighteenth-century English slang word *mud*, which meant "dope" or "fool." The word *mud* was used in this context in the 1800s in relation to any member of the British parliament who lost an election or disgraced himself.

The phrase "the mud press" was also used in the 1840s to refer to scandalous newspapers that defamed people.

WHAT CAUSES PEOPLE TO GO BALD?

Baldness is a condition that plagues many men and some women (and even other primates). The most common form of baldness is a progressive thinning of the hair on the head.

Male pattern balding is said to affect around 66 percent of adult men. Also known as androgenetic alopecia, it is thought to be caused by an enzyme called 5-alpha reductase, which converts testosterone into dihydrotestosterone (DHT) in genetically predisposed men. DHT acts by binding to receptor sites on the cells of the hair follicles to cause specific changes. It inhibits hair growth because healthy hair follicles start producing thinner and more brittle shafts of hair and can even die out. Men bald as they age because it takes time for the susceptible hair follicles to weaken and die. Baldness in women is thought to occur because of a decrease in estrogen, a female hormone that usually balances the balding effect of testosterone.

Many myths are related to baldness, including these: 1. It is caused by intense intellectual activity. This may have been believed because the brain is in the head. 2. It is caused by emotional stress and sexual frustration. Emotional stress can play a role, but sexual frustration is not considered a reason for baldness. 3. Bald men are more virile. This may be believed because some forms of baldness can be prevented by castration. 4. Shaving hair makes it grow back thicker and stronger. This is untrue, as the number and thickness of hairs is governed by the follicles underneath the skin. 5. Baldness is inherited from the mother's side of the family. Genetics plays a role in balding (and the genes for male balding are on the X chromosome), but the relevant genes can come from either parent.

Although there is some disagreement as to the evolutionary basis for baldness, many believe it is due to sexual selection: Baldness is said to indicate maturity and therefore superior nurturing abilities. This may have meant that bald men had a higher status and found it easier to secure partners as they aged.

CAN A CHICKEN RUN WITH ITS HEAD CUT OFF?

The expression "running around like a chicken with its head cut off" refers to someone in a frenzy. The colorful saying prompts many to wonder whether a chicken can actually keep moving once its head has been separated from its body.

It is true that a decapitated chicken can run around for a while. Although the brain is severed from the spinal cord, precluding any voluntary control of movement, electrical impulses from the spinal cord can still cause the chicken to flap its wings and even run. Adrenaline still present in the chicken's muscles also allows this to happen for a short while.

Any such movement by a chicken will usually last for only up to a minute. But in 1945 the locomotion of a chicken in Colorado named Mike lasted a lot longer. In trying to butcher the bird, its owner cut off the chicken's head but the brain stem was left intact. Without a head, Mike was able to balance on a perch and even walk. Mike was fed with an eyedropper, although he would often choke, and his owner would clear the obstruction with a syringe. Mike was taken to shows where people paid to view him. In 1947, he choked and died. It was later determined that the ax had missed Mike's jugular vein and a blood clot had formed, which prevented him from bleeding to death. His intact brain stem allowed his reflexes to operate, which accounted for his movement.

 **WHY DO PEOPLE BLUSH?**

Blushing usually involves a reddening of the face and sometimes an increase in heart rate. It is usually associated with people (especially the young) who become embarrassed or ashamed, and it can occur even when someone is alone. It generally cannot be controlled. Erythrophobia is the pathological fear of blushing.

When a person's mind is confused by embarrassment, the sympathetic nervous system is activated. This stimulates vasodilators, which cause the peripheral capillaries to expand. As a result, more blood flows to the surface of the skin of the face, causing it to turn red.

Some say that when a person blushes, the blood flows to the surface of the entire body but is just more visible on the face because of its structure. Others claim that a specific form of vasodilation occurs on the skin of the face; there is evidence to support this assertion. The facial skin has more capillary loops and vessels than other areas of the skin. The blood vessels in the skin of the face are also wider in diameter and closer to the surface. This makes them more visible when they expand, resulting in a blush.

Only humans blush. It is thought that the reason other animals don't blush is because their brains are not advanced enough to deal with issues of morality.

WHAT IS THE BEST WAY TO TREAT SNAKEBITE?

Throughout the years, there have been a number of recommended first aid methods for treating snakebite. One reason for the inconsistencies is that different methods are used with different types of snake. A method that is effective with one type of snakebite could result in death with another.

However, the following guidelines are now suggested for most bites:

The lymphatic system is responsible for the spread of snakebite venom. This spreading can be reduced or delayed by firmly bandaging the bitten area. Point the bandage toward the central parts of the body. This will help to contain the venom in the bitten area. The bandage should not be so tight as to cut off blood flow. It should not be removed until proper medical attention is received and an antivenin administered.

The limb should be immobilized by applying a sling or splint. The patient should also be immobilized and not allowed to walk or move around. This immobilization will help to prevent the venom from spreading throughout the bloodstream. Coupled with this, the patient should be kept calm to avoid an increase in heart rate.

The patient should receive nothing to eat or drink.

The bite area should not be washed or cut open. It is important for traces of the venom to remain so that medical professionals can determine what antivenin to use. It is thought that washing does not remove much venom anyway, nor does sucking the bite using either a pump or the mouth. This should not be done—to do so could be dangerous to the caregiver.

A tourniquet should not be applied. This was the old approach, but it prevents blood flow to the area and stops the natural dissipation of the venom. This can increase its damaging effects. For the same reason, ice should not be applied to the bite.

❓ HOW DO HOVERCRAFTS WORK?

A hovercraft is an amphibian-style vehicle that can traverse a multitude of terrains. It can travel over grass, mud, water, snow, and ice, making it an extremely versatile machine. Although it prefers gentle terrain, it is capable of climbing slopes.

The vehicle was designed in 1716 by the Swede Emanuel Swedenborg, although that vehicle needed deep water and could not transition from water to land. Then in 1877 a British engineer, Sir John Thornycroft, built a model based on the concept of using air between the hull of a boat and the water. Christopher Cockerell designed the first practical hovercraft in 1952.

Hovercrafts work on the principles of propulsion and lift. They generally have two engines, which drive the fans. One provides forward thrust and the other lifts the hovercraft by forcing air underneath it through a hole in the craft. The basic principle of the hovercraft is that the vehicle is supported by a cushion of air ejected against the surface that the vehicle is traveling across, meaning the craft has virtually no contact with the surface. This lift allows the hovercraft to travel on a cushion of air a few inches off the ground. The air that is forced out to give lift is kept locked in by a skirt, which is a flexible piece of material that contains enough pressure under the craft to lift it. The correct amount of airflow must be maintained to keep the craft stable and prevent it from flipping over. The large base area of the craft also adds to its stability. Rudders are used to direct the hovercraft. The rudders move the thrusting air, which dictates the direction of the hovercraft.

The hovercraft is a very efficient vehicle because the cushion of air means that there is little friction to slow the craft. Thus only a small amount of power is required to move it.

HOW WAS THE GREAT PYRAMID OF EGYPT BUILT?

The Great Pyramid of Giza in Egypt is the only remaining relic of the Seven Wonders of the Ancient World. Also known as the Pyramid of Khufu, it was the tomb of the Egyptian king Khufu. Situated near modern-day Cairo, Egypt, its completion date is estimated to be around 2580 BC. When built, the Great Pyramid was 480 feet (146 meters) high, and its base covered 13 acres (5.3 hectares). It was constructed

from blocks of basalt and granite weighing up to 4 tons, with some blocks on the inside of the pyramid weighing 80 tons. The total mass of blocks is estimated at 5.9 million tons, and the pyramid's volume is estimated to be more than 88 million cubic feet (2.5 million cubic meters). It was originally finished with blocks of polished limestone and was visible from mountains up to two hundred miles away.

The pyramid was perfectly smooth and built with nearly absolute accuracy. The four sides of the base form an almost flawless square, with a mean error of only 50 millimeters in length and 12 seconds in angle. The sides are almost exactly aligned with the four points of the compass. The stones of the pyramid fit together impeccably, and the pyramid contains many passages and three chambers, the latter arranged on the vertical axis of the pyramid. Modern technology cannot construct a monument with the precision of the Great Pyramid, and many question how it was built.

For centuries, archaeologists believed that the pyramid was built by armies of slaves; perhaps as many as 300,000 slaves in a 20-year period. As many as 25 men would have been needed to move any of the 2-ton blocks. Evidence from the tombs now suggests that the pyramid was built not by slaves but by highly skilled craftspeople, who were paid and lived in a city in Giza. Some think the stones from a nearby quarry were moved and affixed using wooden scaffolding or a series of spiraling ramps. Sleds might also have been used to transport the stones. And wind power might have been exploited in the form of kites and pulleys.

It is likely that we will never know who built the Great Pyramid or how, but it is considered by all to be an extraordinary feat of architecture and construction that might never be rivaled.

? WHAT LED TO THE Y2K HYSTERIA?

The Y2K bug (also known as the millennium bug or the year 2000 problem) caused mass hysteria during the late 1990s. Because of a flaw in the programming of computers, many believed that January 1, 2000, would usher in disaster.

The flaw related to computers being unable to process dates once the year read 2000. It was thought that computers would cease to work or would produce incorrect results because they stored dates using only two digits, so "00" might be read as "1900" instead of "2000." This two-digit programming design was created in the 1960s, when computer memories were far smaller and could not cope with large amounts of data. The programs at the time were often for single, short-term incidents, and it was not thought that they would be used for decades. Despite reports in the 1970s of a potential future problem, these warnings weren't acted upon until the 1990s.

People feared that electrical and financial industries would malfunction, planes would crash, and even nuclear bombs would be launched. The media fueled these concerns with a great deal of publicity about the issue. Governments and companies worldwide undertook extensive testing in the 1990s in an attempt to avert the inevitable crisis. Reports of testing that yielded mixed and uncertain results added to the concern. Massive amounts of money were spent before 2000 attempting to remedy the Y2K bug. Some individuals stockpiled large amounts of canned food and supplies to combat the crash. Insurance companies sold policies to cover the failure of businesses because of Y2K. On the eve of 2000, the US military and the Russian military had teams in place in case disaster struck.

As it turned out, there was no significant global computer crash on January 1, 2000, and people's fears were allayed with the passing of the date. There were some mishaps—a nuclear power plant in Japan shut down for a short period, some satellites malfunctioned temporarily, and Norway's rail system shut down—but in most cases the problems were minimal and easily rectified.

HOW ARE 3-D MOVIES MADE?

A 3-D film uses two-dimensional pictures to create the illusion of depth (that is, a third dimension).

Popularly considered to be a modern invention, 3-D movies have actually been in existence for more than 100 years. Although 3-D film was shown in public for the first time at the 1903 Paris World's Fair, the concept is thought to have been invented in the 1800s. The 1903 film lasted one minute and could be viewed only through a type of stereoscope and by only one person at a time, The 1950s saw a fad for 3-D movies, and 3-D films became popular once again in the 1980s. Today, when maximum dramatic impact is desired, a 3-D movie is shown on an enormous IMAX theater screen.

A 3-D film is made by taking two identical images and placing them next to each other at different angles. When viewed in such a way that each eye sees only the image adjacent to it, the human brain interprets the two images as one three-dimensional image. 3-D glasses are sometimes used to filter the two images so that each image enters only one eye, creating a 3-D effect.

Binoculars work on a similar principle by presenting each eye with a slightly different image so that the eyes seem to see depth.

Not confined to movies, 3-D imaging is also used for a number of scientific and military purposes, including examining aerial images depicting the topography of landscapes.

⁇ DID THOMAS CRAPPER INVENT THE TOILET?

Thomas Crapper lived from 1836 to 1910 and founded Thomas Crapper & Co. Ltd. in London. It is often claimed that Crapper invented the flush toilet. This is an urban myth, fueled by the Wallace Reyburn 1969 biography, *Flushed with Pride: The Story of Thomas Crapper*.

The flush toilet was actually invented by Sir John Harington in 1596. Crapper was a plumber and did a lot to popularize this toilet. He promoted sanitary plumbing and in 1880 provided

Prince Edward (who later became King Edward VII) with plumbing and 30 toilets, for which Crapper received a royal warrant, allowing him to supply the British royal family.

Crapper held patents on toilets and plumbing, and some of his advertising implied that he had invented the flush toilet. An 1898 patent was called Crapper's valveless water waste preventer. This patent, however, was not his; it belonged to Albert Giblin.

The word *crap*, from Middle English, means "residue" or "dregs." The connection between Thomas Crapper's plumbing career and his surname is coincidental. Using the word *crapper* to mean "toilet" first occurred in the 1930s. Some believe that US soldiers stationed in England during World War I saw toilets with T. Crapper printed on them and took the word home, where it became a commonplace (and vulgar) reference to the toilet.

WHY DO PEOPLE GET GOOSE BUMPS?

Nearly everyone gets goose bumps from time to time, usually when cold, apprehensive, or afraid. Goose bumps are an automatic emotional or physical response that we normally can't control.

Also known as cutes anserinae, goose bumps are the tiny lumps that appear on a person's skin at the base of the hairs. They are caused by a reflex called piloerection, and are named after the skin of a plucked goose. Piloerection occurs when the muscles at the base of each hair contract and pull the hair erect. The piloerection reflex is governed by the sympathetic nervous system, which is responsible for the fight-or-flight reaction. Once a particular stimulus occurs, nerves discharge, causing the muscles to contract and the hairs to stand on end.

Goose bumps also occur in other animals and are responsible for making cold animals warm or scared animals more impressive looking. When the hairs stand on end, the body is more insulated against the cold because a layer of air becomes trapped under the hairs. An animal will also appear larger and more intimidating to enemies when its hairs stand erect. An example is the porcupine, whose quills stand on end when it is threatened. Some experts believe that goose bumps also provide additional blood to the muscles to assist with the fight-or-flight reaction.

Humans now have minimal body hair, so goose bumps serve no known purpose. They are a vestigial trait from the days of our hair-covered ancestors.

WHY ARE HORSESHOES CONSIDERED LUCKY?

For centuries, the horseshoe has been held to be a good luck charm. A horseshoe hanging in a house has been thought to protect the inhabitants and provide them with good fortune.

The belief seems to have its origin in AD 959, when Saint Dunstan, who became the archbishop of Canterbury, is said to have nailed a horseshoe to the devil's horse. The devil promised to never enter a place where a horseshoe was hung over the door. Horseshoes were also thought to bring good luck because blacksmiths made them. Because blacksmiths worked with fire and iron, they were thought by some to possess special powers. This was because iron was considered magical due to its ability to withstand fire. It is stronger than other metals and was believed to be a charm to ward off evil spirits. Some even believed that blacksmiths could heal the sick.

Folk magic also dictated that a horseshoe nailed above a doorway prevented witches from entering. Similarly, a horseshoe nailed over a bed was thought to repel demons and nightmares. Folklore stated that, once affixed, the horseshoe must never be removed.

Today, the horseshoe is still considered a lucky charm. Different cultures hold different superstitions about how the

horseshoe is hung. A common belief is that for good luck the two ends of the horseshoe must point upward. This prevents the good luck from draining out. However, in some regions the ends must point down so that the good luck pours on to the recipient. In some traditions, the good luck occurs only for the owner of the horseshoe; other traditions require the horseshoe to be found in order to be effective.

HAS ANY HUMAN BEEN SUCCESSFULLY RAISED BY ANIMALS?

In the world of literature, several fictional characters have been raised by animals, most notably, Tarzan in a series of novels by Edgar Rice Burroughs and Mowgli in Rudyard Kipling's *Jungle Book* series.

In real life, there have been around 100 instances of children being raised by or living with animals. They are often called feral children, having lived away from humans due to being abandoned or lost in the wild.

The first famous feral child was Peter the Wild Boy, who was found in Hanover, Germany, in 1724 at the age of 12. He was ragged, would climb trees and eat plants, and never learned to speak. Feral children often have difficulty mastering language and fitting into society. Other, less-documented examples are the Hessian wolf-children, found in 1341; the Lithuanian bear-boys, discovered in the 1600s; and the young girls Kamala and Amala, who were discovered in 1920 and said to have been raised by wolves in India.

A more recent case was Oxana Malaya, who was born in 1983 and found at the age of eight in the Ukraine. Because Oxana's alcoholic parents could not care for her adequately, she had lived in a kennel behind her house with a pack of dogs for most of her young life. She had been cared for by the dogs and developed dog-like mannerisms and behavioral patterns. She crouched, barked, and growled, as well as smelled her food before eating it. She had extremely acute senses of hearing, sight, and smell. After she was discovered, she lived in a facility for disabled people, where she found social interaction and learning language skills very difficult.

These remarkable accounts illustrate that it is possible for animals to raise and care for people in a manner similar to the story of Tarzan.

❓ WHY ARE MOST BARNS IN AMERICA RED?

In rural United States, nearly all farms have barns to house animals, machinery, or feed for stock. Many of these barns, particularly in New England and New York state, are painted red. Some wonder about this uniformity of color.

In the 1800s, when most barns were built, many rural families were poor. Painting for aesthetics was considered a luxury, but painting was often necessary to protect wood from the elements.

At the time, ferric oxide was one of the cheapest and most readily available chemicals for farmers. Ferric oxide was red and early American farmers used it to make their own paint. When the ferric oxide was mixed with other

ingredients, such as milk, lime, and linseed oil, the presence of this chemical yielded a red paint. It was this paint that was used on the barns.

Many modern-day barns are red, continuing the tradition. In some poorer areas, such as parts of the South, barns are often left unpainted. More affluent areas, which raise horses and purebred livestock, have barns of yellow, white, or green. Farms with barns of these colors are often found in Virginia, Kentucky, and Pennsylvania.

IS *JURASSIC PARK* POSSIBLE?

In the 1993 movie *Jurassic Park*, dinosaurs are cloned from DNA found in mosquitoes that have been preserved for millions of years. The dinosaur DNA is spliced with frog DNA to make it complete and placed in ostrich eggs, out of which hatch dinosaurs. There are many compelling reasons why this process could not work and why the cloning of dinosaurs is not possible.

The dinosaur DNA would be mixed with mosquito DNA, which might contain DNA from a number of species of dinosaur, meaning replication of a single species would not be possible. In any event, enzymes in the mosquitoes would break down the dinosaur DNA, so the mosquitoes would need to be preserved immediately after feeding on dinosaur blood.

Although dinosaur DNA has been found in real life, it is always broken apart and needs to be sequenced. This cannot be done, as there are no complete strands of dinosaur DNA available to copy. Even if it was sequenced, dinosaur DNA would have gaps. Every chromosome must be present, and this is never the case with DNA that has been preserved for millions of years. The fossilization process alters molecules in the DNA. These gaps in the dinosaur DNA cannot be filled by splicing dinosaur DNA with frog DNA, as this process would not produce a dinosaur. And even if sequenced and complete dinosaur DNA was available, it would need to be inserted into an oocyte (a female germ cell, which gives rise to an ovum) from a dinosaur. As no dinosaurs now exist, there are no dinosaur oocytes. If all of these factors were present, a dinosaur egg would be needed from which to hatch the dinosaur. Only a dinosaur egg could provide the hormones and other nutrients to nourish a dinosaur.

These numerous factors mean that with today's technology, cloning dinosaurs is impossible.

WHY DOES HELIUM ALTER THE HUMAN VOICE?

A common party trick among children is to breathe in the gas from a helium-filled balloon and then talk in a high-pitched, squeaky voice like a cartoon character.

The human voice is produced by resonating sound waves in the throat and mouth. The wavelengths of these sound waves are fixed inside the throat and mouth. Helium is an inert gas that is lighter than air. (Hydrogen is the only gas that's lighter, and it's extremely flammable.) Because helium is lighter than air, it has a greater velocity than air at the same temperature, which means that the speed of sound in helium is faster than in oxygen. If a gas of a higher velocity is used when the wavelengths of the sounds are constant, the result is a higher frequency. This higher frequency shapes the voice so that a higher-pitched sound is produced.

Interestingly, sulfur hexafluoride has the opposite effect of helium, slowing down the speed of sound and making the voice lower.

If inhaled to excess, helium can be dangerous. Although helium is not toxic, by breathing it in, the body is deprived of oxygen. In extreme cases, this lack of oxygen leads to unconsciousness, brain damage, or even death. Another potential side effect of inhaling helium is ruptured lungs if the gas is inhaled directly from a high-pressure gas cylinder.

HOW DOES ACUPUNCTURE WORK?

Acupuncture is an alternative medical practice that involves inserting small needles into specific points on the body in an attempt to heal or alleviate symptoms of illness. It has been practiced in China since 1000 BC and is still very popular today.

The theory of acupuncture is that the human body has "systems of function." Disease is said to alter one or more of these. Acupuncture treats the disease by changing the activity in the systems of function through the insertion of needles on particular acupuncture points. There are said to be 12 primary channels, or meridians, which run across the body, creating a kind of map. Meridians are either yin (female, dark, and passive) or yang (male, light, and active) and correspond with different organs. For example, the three yin channels of the foot travel from the foot to the chest and correspond with the spleen, kidney, and liver. The body's vital energy, known as chi, travels along the meridians, and pain is said to be caused by a deficiency or imbalance of chi. Acupuncture works to relieve pain through the regulation of the flow of chi, achieved by inserting the needles in particular places along the meridians. One traditional acupuncture point is the lung meridian, which is situated on the inside of the wrist. This point is used to treat various ailments, including asthma and coughing.

Although many people swear by it, acupuncture has no modern medical basis and is widely criticized as a pseudoscience. For example, there is no physical evidence for the existence of chi. Indeed, the *British Medical Journal* reports that needles inserted at random on certain patients are just as effective as needles inserted on designated acupuncture points. However, a 1997 report by the National Institutes of Health in Britain found that there is sufficient evidence of acupuncture's value to expand its use into conventional medicine.

WHY IS ROUTE 66 FAMOUS?

Route 66 was a US highway that conjured up images of romance and freedom. It traversed an enormous part of America, running a total distance of 2,448 miles. Beginning in Chicago, it ran through the states of Missouri, Kansas, Oklahoma, Texas, New Mexico, Arizona, and California, ending at the Santa Monica beach.

The idea for Route 66 began with Cyrus Avery in 1923; the road was completed in 1938. Avery was a member of the board appointed to create the Federal Highway System. Originally to be named Route 60, other members from

Kentucky wanted a Virginia Beach–to–Los Angeles road to be US 60, so Avery settled on Route 66 because he thought an even, two-digit number would be easy to remember.

Route 66 was designed to link many towns throughout America. It was a popular truck route, which increased industry throughout the country. This was unlike all other roads in America at the time, which did not follow a diagonal course. The highway became the major route taken by families in drought-stricken Oklahoma in the 1930s, who headed west to make a new start. It is estimated that more than 200,000 people used the route for this purpose, and it was viewed as the "road to opportunity." It was also extensively used by American soldiers returning from World War II, who traveled Route 66 to visit their families and for vacations. The popularity of the route dramatically increased tourism and gave birth to roadside attractions, motels, and fast-food outlets. The first McDonald's restaurant was on Route 66 at San Bernardino.

Officially decommissioned as a highway in 1985, it is still followed by many people, including tourists from around the world, because of the nostalgia associated with the road. Route 66 associations were set up in 1990, and Missouri declared its section of the road a State Historic Route. Signs announcing this line the entire length of the road in that state. Still famous to this day, Route 66 symbolized the spirit of hope and optimism in America and was romanticized in John Steinbeck's 1946 novel *The Grapes of Wrath*, in which he referred to it as "the road of flight" and the "Mother Road." It also inspired songs, such as "(Get Your Kicks On) Route 66," as well as the television program *Route 66*.

HOW DOES VENTRILOQUISM WORK?

Ventriloquism (which the ancient Greeks called gastromancy) is a skill that a ventriloquist uses, manipulating his or her voice to make it seem as if it were coming from somewhere else.

The art has been in existence for thousands of years. It is thought that in ancient times ventriloquism was related to wizardry and black magic, and was used by the chiefs of tribes to communicate with supernatural powers. It is also thought to have been used by some cultures in religious ceremonies. Some believe that "possessed" people in the Bible were nothing more than ventriloquists.

In the twentieth century, ventriloquism developed into the comedy routine that we see today—where a performer sits with a dummy on his or her lap and has a mock conversation with it.

It is a fallacy that a ventriloquist can throw the voice. The aim of the ventriloquist is to give the impression to the audience that the voice is being thrown. Creating this illusion depends on a number of factors.

The sense of hearing is one of the easiest to deceive, and a ventriloquist attempts to misdirect the listener's ear. To achieve this, the ventriloquist manipulates the dummy to ensure that it opens its mouth in time with the words that the ventriloquist speaks. The brain of the listener then makes the natural connection that the dummy is actually talking. The movements of the lips of the ventriloquist are kept to an absolute minimum to increase the illusion. Many words can be said in this way with ease, although some require a great deal of practice. The other skill that a ventriloquist uses is to keep the dummy in constant motion, creating the illusion of life and drawing the listener's eyes to the dummy. To increase the dummy's lifelike appearance, a ventriloquist might give the dummy a personality that is different from the ventriloquist's to make the dummy unique and appealing to the audience.

WHY ARE CHILDREN'S COIN BANKS CALLED PIGGY BANKS?

A piggy bank is a traditional container, used mainly by children, in which to store coins. Piggy banks are often shaped like pigs, yet, contrary to popular belief, the name is not derived from *pig*.

Although the exact origin of the piggy bank is not clear, historians believe that it was first used in the Middle Ages in England. In the 1500s, people often kept coins in "pygg jars." Metal was expensive and pygg was a cheap clay used for making household objects, such as jars and pots.

By the 1700s, *pygg* was pronounced *pig*, and it is likely that potters who received requests to make pygg jars or banks mistakenly made them in the shape of a pig.

The comically shaped coin banks appealed to children, and they are still favorites today.

WHY IS CHICAGO KNOWN AS THE "WINDY CITY"?

Chicago is dubbed the "Windy City." There are a couple of conflicting stories about the origin of this nickname.

It is often said that the name comes from the long-winded, boastful speeches of Chicago politicians. Shortly before the World's Columbian Exhibition of 1893, the people of Chicago were staking a claim to host the exhibition. New York was in competition with Chicago, and Charles Dana from the *New York Sun* newspaper wrote an editorial telling New Yorkers to dismiss the "nonsensical claims of that windy city." But despite common belief, this is not the origin of the name.

Earlier references to this nickname have been found. In 1886, the *Chicago Tribune* called the town the "Windy City" because of the refreshing lake breezes of the summer resorts. Prior to this time, the city was known as the "Garden City"; it is thought that the name was changed around 1880. Another reference to the "Windy City" exists in an 1885 edition of the *Cleveland Gazette*, although the reason for the nickname is not explained. Other unexplained references have been found in the early 1880s, and it is likely that the theory of refreshing lake breezes is correct.

 HOW DO BIRDS MIGRATE?

Many species of bird migrate at different times of the year to seek better feeding grounds, to find a safer place to breed, or to avoid a harsh climate. Some birds travel enormous distances, flying up to 400 miles per day. The arctic tern flies 11,000 miles to reach its migration destination. To prepare for a journey, most species will eat extra food to increase fat reserves and to ensure their feathers are strong for the flight. But how birds manage to find their way over such long distances is a more perplexing question.

Scientists believe that birds use several skills to help them migrate. Some birds are thought to use landmarks (such as rivers and mountains) to navigate, while others use wind direction and thermal columns of hot air to direct them. Sounds such as waves on shores and winds through mountains are also believed to be used, as are different smells.

Many ornithological experts now believe that most birds navigate using Earth's magnetic field, as well as the stars and the sun. The sun is thought to be used by some birds, while experiments have shown that others use the stars. It is thought that birds orient themselves to the compass points using the position of the sun in the day and the stars at night. One experiment showed that birds who had been reared in cages and had never seen the sky were observed to use the stars to navigate. Birds will often stop migrating on cloudy nights. Some birds are also believed to recalibrate their built-in magnetic compasses against the sun and stars during periods of rest.

Many think that birds have a built-in sense of direction and innately know where to go. This is seen in the young of many birds, who are on their own early in life but migrate without any training.

WHAT ARE THE POKER HAND RANKINGS?

Poker is one of the most popular card games. Hundreds of high-stakes tournaments are held worldwide, and the advent of online poker has attracted millions to the cyber table. The poker winner is decided according to what five-card hand each player holds. There are more than 2.5 million different five-card hands possible, and they are

ranked in order of the following hierarchy (because the probability of the best hands occurring is lowest). There is no ranking of suits in poker, so a particular hand consisting of all spades is equal to the same hand of all clubs, and the players split the pot.

Royal flush—The ultimate hand, it consists of ace, king, queen, jack, and ten, all in the same suit.

Straight flush—Any five cards in sequence and in the same suit, for example, jack, ten, nine, eight, seven. When two players have this, the higher individual card wins. This rule applies to all hands in poker (in some cases, the highest pair wins, and if they are equal, the second-highest pair, followed by the lowest card, if all else is equal).

Four of a kind—Four cards of the same value plus another card, for example, four tens and one two.

Full house—Three cards of the same value and two cards of another value, for example, three sixes and two nines. This is ranked by the highest three of a kind, so that 66622 beats 555KK.

Flush—Any five cards of the same suit.

Straight—Any five cards in sequence but not all of the same suit. The ace can be used to be higher than the king or lower than the two.

Three of a kind—The same as "four of a kind," except only three cards are of the same value.

Two pair—Two cards of one value and two of another, for example, two fives and two eights.

One pair—Two cards of one value.

No pair—No pair and the cards are ranked in order of seniority (A, K, Q, J, 10 to 2).

HOW DID THE EXPRESSION "RIDING SHOTGUN" BEGIN?

The expression "riding shotgun" means sitting in the front passenger seat of a car or other vehicle.

It is commonly thought that the origin of the expression is from the days of the stagecoach. On stagecoaches, an armed man would often sit in the passenger seat next to the driver to protect against such perils as Indians and robbers.

The word *shotgun* has existed since the 1700s to refer to a gun that shoots a load of shots instead of a single bullet. The scattering of the pellets makes it more likely that the intended target will be hit. It is ideal for shooting in close quarters, where taking steady aim is often impossible. Indeed, evidence shows that shotguns were often the weapon of choice of the men riding shotgun on the stagecoaches in the late 1800s.

Although men did ride shotgun in the stagecoach days of the West, there is no evidence that the expression existed in that time. It is believed that the phrase was first used in the twentieth century in movies about the West. The 1939 movie *Stagecoach* refers to the expression.

The idea of riding shotgun in an automobile (when in fact not carrying a shotgun) first appeared in the 1960s. The person who wanted to lay claim to the passenger seat of a car would "call shotgun." As time passed, so-called urban rules were created for calling shotgun. For example, it could be called only if the prospective passengers were within a certain short distance of the car, with various reciprocal deals often made between auto owners who frequently carpooled together.

❓ HOW DO BEES NAVIGATE?

For years, scientists have studied how bees get around. Typically, a bee travels in an irregular path to a food source (which may be up to 6 miles away) and then returns to the hive in a straight line. After the bee performs a dance (a circular pattern with an occasional zigzag) at the hive, other bees make their way to that food source in a straight line.

Studies show that bees are adept learners. If a particular plant produces nectar, a bee will return to it, ignoring other, less nourishing plants. An experiment in which bees were trained to negotiate a maze indicated their learning abilities. Although most experts agree that bees are able to learn, there is much conjecture as to how bees find their way and the relevance of their peculiar dance.

Some argue that bees use odor and their acute sense of smell, as well as various landmarks on their route, to guide them. They say that the dance alerts the remaining bees to the particular odor, which they then follow to the source. Others believe that bees possess a maplike spatial memory, which they use to navigate.

Many experts now believe that bees use the sun as a reference point when navigating. It is thought that bees use the sun as a relatively stationary point and orient themselves by maintaining a fixed angle relative to the sun. These experts believe that the dance performed by a bee directs the other bees to the food by reference to the sun, indicating the angle relative to the sun that the other bees should follow.

❓ WHY DOES PASTA WATER FOAM?

As any cook will agree, when pasta is boiled it produces a foam, which often boils over the pot and on to the stove.

The intense heat of the boiling water is needed to "set" the pasta and prevent it from sticking together. However, when added to boiling water, pasta begins to break down and release a starchy substance. This is because pasta contains starch molecules, which are freed with boiling. Once released, the starch  molecules interfere with the water molecules on the surface of the water, making it easier for foam to form. The starchy substance then produces the foamy bubbles that form on the top and edge of the pot. The freed starch molecules form networks and thicken the water, creating the bubbly foam.

Adding a small amount of oil to the boiling water before the pasta is added will minimize the starchy foam and coat the pasta with oil. Adding oil also prevents the pieces from sticking together, as does stirring the pasta while it cooks. Using plenty of water to begin with also helps to keep the pieces of pasta separate.

❓ WHY DO CATS PURR?

Many species of cat purr. Purring is a buzzing sound that can cause the cat's whole body to shake. The loudness and intensity of the purr varies from species to species and from cat to cat. Some scientists believe that cats purr by using a set of "false" vocal cords, which have no other purpose. Others believe that purring is caused by blood vibrating against the aorta. Still others think it's from the movement of air caused by contractions in the diaphragm.

It is thought that cats purr for many different reasons. Many believe that purring indicates a friendly, social, and contented mood. This is because cats often purr when stroked. However, cats also purr when they are frightened or uneasy. If a cat is in pain or injured, it will also often purr. Some believe cats purr during times of hardship as a means of comforting themselves or signaling that they need attention, either physical or emotional. Cats may also purr when injured as a means of reducing pain and even as a healing mechanism. Cats purr while giving birth, which may be to reduce the pain. Because the sound frequencies of a typical cat purr are known to increase bone density in people, some believe cats purr to keep their bones strong.

Scientists believe that cats use purring as a form of communication between mother and kitten. Although a newborn kitten's senses are not acute, it can feel the vibrations of its mother's purr.

WHAT IS THE ORIGIN OF THE WEREWOLF LEGEND?

A werewolf is a mythological person who turns into a wolf. This transformation is said to occur when there is a full moon and a curse has been placed on the person or when the person has previously been bitten by a wolf. The legend of the werewolf has been popularized in films. The word *werewolf* is thought to be derived from a number of different old languages in which a word similar to *were* means "a man." Another theory is that the word is derived from the Old English word *weir*, which means "to wear," and thus a werewolf is someone who wears a wolf's skin.

Many European cultures have stories of werewolves. In Greek mythology, Lycaon became a wolf after eating human flesh. In Norse mythology, berserkers were fighters who dressed in wolfskins. The French, too, have many accounts of werewolves, including the Beast of Gevaudan, which was described in the 1760s as a giant wolf that attacked livestock as well as people.

Although many countries have their own werewolf story, it is thought that the legend began in 1591 near the German towns of Cologne and Bedburg. Wolf attacks on people were frequent, and landowners regularly tried to kill the wolves. Legend has it that a wolf was cornered one day but, despite being hit by sticks, did not run. The wolf then stood up and revealed himself to be a man, Peter Stubbe, from a nearby village. Stubbe was tortured and confessed to 16 savage murders. His head was removed and placed on a tall pole. It had the likeness of a wolf, and people began to believe that werewolves lived among them.

Some researchers have explained the werewolf phenomenon by pointing out that eating a particular fungus that grew in Europe in the Middle Ages resulted in hallucinations and paranoia. Rabies, as well as hypertrichosis—a condition that results in excessive hair growth over the entire body—have also been cited as origins of the myth of the werewolf.

The legend of the werewolf continues to this day. In the late 1990s in India, werewolves were blamed for a spate of wolf attacks on humans.

WHAT LED TO THE DOWNFALL OF COMMUNISM?

Communism is a political system based on the communal ownership of all property and means of production. It existed in the Soviet Union, Eastern Europe, Cuba, and parts of Asia during much of the twentieth century. Communist regimes were powerful and the Soviet Union was one of the world's superpowers. But in 1991, communism ended in the Soviet Union and Eastern Europe (although it still exists to a degree in China, other parts of Asia, and Cuba).

European communism declined rapidly in the 1980s. Democracy was a powerful force in the Western world, and this information began filtering into the Communist states. In 1985, Mikhail Gorbachev became the leader of the Soviet Union. He introduced massive economic reforms, including his program of perestroika, a system of restructuring aimed to enhance and modernize society. He allowed cooperatives and family businesses to form, as well as permitted farmers to sell produce on the open market. He also relaxed foreign trade restrictions and foreign investment in the country.

Gorbachev also introduced social and political reforms with his program of glasnost, a policy of openness in relation to public affairs. Censorship in the media was relaxed and a ban on associations lifted. He also reduced Soviet military spending and negotiated an end to the Cold War with the West. In 1988, he provided for competition in business and multicandidate elections for many forms of government throughout the Soviet Union. By 1990, non-Communist political parties were allowed to propose candidates to run in elections. Powerful public figures began demanding a democratic state. Nationalist sentiment increased in countries where economic conditions had worsened since Gorbachev's policies had taken effect, and the Soviet Union did not intervene when several countries, including Poland, East Germany, Czechoslovakia, and Bulgaria, abandoned Communist rule.

An attempted coup in 1991 tried to turn Gorbachev into a figurehead leader. It failed but Gorbachev's position had been compromised. In that year the Communist Party was banned in Russia and Gorbachev resigned. The Soviet Union ceased to exist, and communism in Europe was over.

WHAT ARE THE SEVEN WONDERS OF THE NATURAL WORLD?

With the Seven Wonders of the Ancient World destroyed (with the exception of the Great Pyramid), people began searching for other wonders. The Seven Wonders of the Natural World is one of the results. Although there is some disagreement as to what they should be, there are seven commonly accepted wonders.

The Grand Canyon is a gigantic gorge of the Colorado River in Arizona. It's about 1 mile deep, up to 18 miles wide, and more than 200 miles long. The multicolored rocks show the geological changes that have occurred with time. The first European to see the canyon was the Spanish explorer Francisco Vasquez de Coronado in 1540.

Victoria Falls is a waterfall in the Zambezi River in Africa at the border of Zambia and Zimbabwe with a drop of 420 feet. The falls are enormous and produce a thick mist and a loud roar that can be heard up to 25 miles away. British explorer David Livingstone named the falls after Queen Victoria in 1885.

Mount Everest is a peak in the Himalayan Mountains on the border of Tibet and Nepal. It is the highest peak in the world and was first reached by Sir Edmund Hilary in 1953.

The Great Barrier Reef is the largest coral reef in the world. It is off the coast of Queensland in Australia and is

approximately 1,250 miles long. In some places it is more than 400 feet thick.

The harbor of Rio de Janeiro in Brazil is breathtaking. Surrounded by low mountain ranges, which extend to the waterside, the harbor is very deep, allowing large boats to enter it.

The Paricutin Volcano in Mexico is an active volcano more than 8,000 feet high. It formed from a cornfield in 1943 and grew until 1952, spewing so much lava that it buried the village of Paricutin and the town of San Juan Parangaricutiro.

The northern lights, also called the aurora borealis, are a colorful display of lights that occur at certain times of year in the night sky of the northern hemisphere. They are caused by the interaction of charged solar wind particles with Earth's magnetic field in the upper atmosphere and are most prominent at higher latitudes, near the magnetic poles.

HOW DO LIE DETECTOR TESTS WORK?

A lie detector, or polygraph, is a device for determining whether a person is lying by monitoring his or her physiological reactions. It measures a subject's heart rate, blood pressure, respiratory rate, and skin conductivity (sweating) while he or she is asked a series of questions.

Polygraphs once involved needles scribbling on scrolling paper. Nowadays, they use computers. Several tubes and wires are connected to specific parts of the body to measure the person's reactions. These reactions are then fed to the computer, which produces the results.

A lie detector test usually starts with opening questions, which the examiner uses as control questions. The examiner asks questions to obtain both truthful and false answers, establishing a pattern from which to work. When further questions are asked, if the physiological factors differ from normal levels, it may indicate that the subject is stressed. And stress is associated with deception, although the results are open to interpretation by the examiner.

The effectiveness of polygraph tests is debated. Some claim the tests are accurate in 70 to 90 percent of cases. Critics, however, claim that adverse reactions can be caused by a wide range of emotions, and can be influenced by the way in which the questions are framed. Critics also cite examples of people whose lies were not spotted by the tests, such as Aldrich Ames, a Russian spy. Ames later said that he passed the test by simply relaxing while the questions were being asked.

Polygraph tests are still used by some US government agencies to screen employees, although polygraph evidence is not generally admissible in court. The tests are not commonly used in Europe, where they are considered unreliable.

WHAT ARE THE "BIG FIVE" GAME ANIMALS OF AFRICA?

The "big five" is a term used by tour operators in Africa to refer to the animals that are the most popular to view. The term was coined by hunters, who ranked Africa's five wild animals that were the most prized kills. The difficulty of the hunt was the reason they made the list, not their size. Some large animals, such as the hippopotamus and giraffe, did not make the list. Even today, the big five are synonymous with the romance of Africa, and many travelers consider a trip there to be incomplete without seeing them.

- The lion is the king of the jungle and the largest of the big cats of Africa. A skilled hunter, the lion is one of the world's most successful carnivores. Lions often hunt in a group, or pride.
- The leopard is the most graceful big cat of Africa. Another successful hunter, known for its stealth and hunting alone, the elusive leopard often sleeps in trees.
- The buffalo is very strong and intimidating and is considered the most dangerous of the big five to hunters. A fast short-distance runner with large horns, it is known to charge with fury and often kills lions.
- The elephant is the largest land animal in the world and, although an herbivore, can be aggressive and dangerous. It has a long, prehensile trunk and huge ivory tusks.

- The rhinoceros is another large herbivore with large horns on its snout. Also a fast runner, it has a notoriously bad temper. Rhinoceroses are an endangered species.

? WHAT CAUSES PHANTOM LIMB PAIN IN AMPUTEES?

People who have lost a limb often experience phantom limb pain. Its symptoms include a stabbing, cramping, or burning sensation in the area where the limb once was. Many people report that the pain is made worse by weather changes, anxiety, or fatigue. Cases of it have been reported since 1871, and its exact cause is a mystery to this day.

Once thought to be a psychological condition (with the amputee considered to be unwilling to accept the loss of the limb), most experts now agree that it is physical, although it may be caused by a number of different factors or a combination of factors. This is one reason why it is difficult to treat. Various medications are commonly prescribed.

Most experts agree that phantom limb pain results from the fact that the motor cortex in the brain is mapped out so that specific areas deal with specific body parts. Even when a limb is lost, the cortex continues to "map" the missing part as if it were still there, often causing pain where the limb once was. Some believe that the pain is caused by the loss of nerve activity in the limb, or by the regeneration of nerves that were cut during the amputation. Others believe that the pain results from a lack of input from the limb to the spine, or because of changes in the cortex of the brain.

Some studies have found that people who had pain in a limb prior to its amputation are more likely to experience phantom limb pain, and that if a limb is removed because of a blood clot, the pain is likely to be greater. This is thought to be because a clot reduces oxygen to a limb and damages it. Injuries to the nerve networks that result in the removal of a limb have also been found to increase phantom limb pain.

WHAT IS THE DIFFERENCE BETWEEN FLOTSAM AND JETSAM?

Flotsam and *jetsam* are often used interchangeably to mean goods that have been thrown from a boat, yet they mean different things.

Jetsam is cargo or equipment that has been thrown overboard to lighten a ship's load in a case of distress. This discarded cargo is often found washed ashore, and this too is jetsam. The word *jetsam* is related to the verb *jettison*, which is from the Latin word *jactation*, meaning "to throw."

Flotsam, on the other hand, is wreckage or cargo that remains afloat after a ship has sunk. Unlike jetsam, flotsam is not deliberately thrown overboard. The word *flotsam* more commonly refers to driftwood and debris floating on the ocean, but this is not technically correct. *Flotsam* is from the Old French word *floter*, meaning "to float."

Here are two more maritime words: *ligan* and *derelict*. Ligan is goods that have been tied to a buoy for later retrieval, and derelict is property that has been abandoned at sea with no intention of recovering it.

WHY IS A LEFT-HANDED SPORTSMAN CALLED A SOUTHPAW?

The word *southpaw* is often associated with left-handed sportsmen, especially boxers and baseball pitchers. It is most commonly used in the United States.

Most sports pundits agree that Finley Peter Dunne, a journalist for the *Chicago News*, coined the term in 1885. The Chicago Cubs' home plate was oriented so that a right-handed batter (the most common type) would face east to avoid the afternoon sun in his eyes. This meant that left-handed ("left-pawed") pitchers would throw from the south side of the diamond. These pitchers became known as southpaws.

Although it is generally thought that the term has its origin in baseball, it is now thought that the first recorded use of *southpaw* was actually in 1848, describing the punch of a left-handed boxer, who leads with the right and follows up with the more powerful left. This 1848 reference is long before the beginning of organized professional baseball and is quoted in the *Oxford English Dictionary*.

WHY DO DOGS WALK IN CIRCLES BEFORE LYING DOWN?

Before lying down, a dog will usually walk around in a circle a couple of times. This habit seems to have no purpose and has led people to question why dogs do this.

Scientists believe that this behavior is an instinct retained from the ancestors of domestic dogs. Because wild dogs slept outdoors in an array of places, they would walk in circles to flatten down the ground. This would trample down any vegetation and make the ground more comfortable to lie on.

Another potential reason for this behavior is that because dogs are territorial and their forebears slept in groups, walking in circles before lying down was a way of marking out a dog's territory and making more room for itself.

Others believe dogs' ancestors trampled down long grass so that they were hidden within the rest of the long grass to protect themselves from predators. Yet another theory is that dogs' forebears would dig and then circle in order to partially burrow into the cool soil to escape hot weather.

Although this habit is unnecessary for domesticated dogs, they are following an ancient instinct.

❓ WHAT IS THE ORIGIN OF "SON OF A GUN"?

Like many expressions, the origin of "son of a gun" has a few conflicting explanations.

A popular view is that it is a nautical expression. In the 1800s, it was common for wives or girlfriends (or even prostitutes) to join sailors aboard ship when it was sailing in home waters. The women and sailors would often sleep together on the gun deck, and if a male child was the result, he was known as a "son of a gun." In his 1867 book, *The Sailor's Word Book*, Admiral William Henry Smyth says, "Son of a gun, an epithet conveying contempt in a slight degree, and originally applied to boys born afloat, when women were permitted to accompany their husbands to sea; one admiral declared he literally was thus cradled, under the breast of a gun-carriage."

A related theory is that sailors traveling to the West Indies sometimes raped native women on ships, often between the cannons. A son born as a result was called "a son between the guns."

Another view is that soldiers were called "guns," so it literally meant "son of a military man." Some also say that if a male child was born to a soldier but the child did not know the father's name, this offspring was recorded as A. Gun.

The first known printed reference to the expression was in the newspaper *The British Apollo*, no. 43, 1708, where it stated "You'r (sic) a Son of a Gun". *Gun* in this context is considered a euphemism for an offensive term, such as *bitch*, *whore*, or *bastard*.

WHAT IS LIGHTNING?

Lightning is an electrostatic discharge that occurs naturally during thunderstorms.

Although the causes of lightning have been debated for years, it is generally thought that droplets of ice and rain become electrically polarized as they pass through the electrical field of the atmosphere. Ice particles can also become charged by electrostatic induction. Once charged, the positively charged crystals rise to the top of a cloud, while the negative ones drop to the bottom of a cloud.

When the field of energy between the two ends of the cloud becomes strong enough, a small electrical discharge, or stepped leader, starts traveling from the cloud to the ground (or to another cloud), moving down in progressive steps. Once it is close to the ground, a small discharge comes up from the ground (or a tall object on it, such as a tree). This closes the circuit, which causes a larger discharge, in the form of a bolt of lightning, to strike. The associated thunder is from the shock waves formed by the rapid heating and expanding of the air along the path of the current. Most lightning is negative, meaning the stepped leader is negatively charged and the discharge from the ground is positive.

The average bolt of lightning has a current of 300,000 amperes (300 kiloamperes) and could power a 100-watt lightbulb for 95 years. A bolt of lightning can also reach temperatures that are five times hotter than the surface of the sun.

Around two thousand people per year are injured by lightning, with about one-third of them dying, usually from damage to the lungs, circulatory system, or central nervous system. Many die from an immediate cardiac arrest.

The expression "lightning never strikes twice" (in the same place) is incorrect: Because of its height and the metal antenna it has, the Empire State Building in New York generally gets hit 25 times every year.

WHAT MAKES PEOPLE'S JOINTS CLICK?

When people walk or run, it is common for the joints in their hips or legs to make a clicking sound. It can also occur when people stretch, and some can even purposely make the noise with their fingers. But what causes this clicking sound?

The joints are supported by an array of muscles, tendons, and ligaments, which keep the joints stable. If the tendons or ligaments are out of alignment or slightly lax, the movement of a ligament from one position to another can cause clicking. An example of this is when a ligament flicks over a bone. The click is actually the iliotibial band moving over the trochanter. A minor strain in the joint can also cause this.

Another reason for the clicking could be the formation of a vacuum when the joint and muscles move. This vacuum can rapidly fill with gas, forming a bubble that replaces the vacuum. This can cause the joint to click when the joint is then moved. Because it takes a while for the gas to be reabsorbed, the same joint cannot normally be clicked again for a short while.

Most medical professionals agree that, provided there is no pain or swelling associated with the clicking, it is nothing to worry about and can be ignored.

 WHAT IS THE BIG BANG THEORY?

For many years, scientists have pondered how the universe was created. The most commonly held theory is the big bang theory. It states that the universe originated from an enormously dense and hot state about 14 billion years ago. From this original state, according to certain technical laws and models (Lemaitre's, Hubble's, and Friedmann's, to name a few), the universe has expanded over time.

The theory is based on observations as well as theories, and in 1927 it was first proposed by Georges Lemaitre that the universe began with an enormous explosion of a "primeval atom." In 1929, Edwin Hubble corroborated this when he observed that the galaxies are moving away from Earth in every direction at speeds relative to their distance from Earth.

Further research, based on the measurements of cosmic microwave background, and the correlation function of galaxies, led cosmologists to agree that the universe does have a finite age. Improvements in telescopes in recent years have led to findings that also indicate that the universe is expanding. In fact, it appears to be expanding at an accelerated rate. Recent measured abundances of light elements (such as baryons and photons) also suggest that the big bang theory is correct, as it is thought that the abundances could not otherwise exist.

Skeptics of the theory cite three main technical issues for their disbelief: the horizon problem, the flatness problem, and the magnetic monopole problem. Despite this criticism, the big bang theory is now well established in cosmology, and its credibility is thought by many to be limited only by the power of current technology. A number of major Christian churches accept the big bang theory of the creation of the universe.

WHY IS WALKING UNDER A LADDER CONSIDERED BAD LUCK?

It is a common superstition that anyone who walks under a ladder will experience bad luck. Some people go to great lengths to avoid doing it.

One theory of the origin of the superstition dates back to the Middle Ages. In England and France in the 1600s, criminals heading for the gallows were forced to walk underneath the ladder that they then climbed to be killed. The executioner would not walk under the ladder but would walk around it instead. Thus walking under a ladder came to be feared; it was as if a person were acting out his or her own execution.

Another explanation is that the triangle formed by a ladder (when either erect or leaning up against a wall) was seen as representing the Holy Trinity. To walk under the ladder and through the triangle was thought to desecrate this symbol, leaving the offender to fall victim to the devil.

Some countermeasures are said to prevent bad luck if you have the misfortune to walk under a ladder: Cross your fingers until you see a dog, spit through the rungs of the ladder three times, or walk backward under the ladder while you make a wish.

WHAT ARE THE ORIGINS OF THE STRIP IN LAS VEGAS?

Las Vegas is a world-famous gambling city, situated in the desert of Nevada. It is most famous for The Strip, which runs for 4 miles on Las Vegas Boulevard South. At the southern end of The Strip is a sign that reads "Welcome to Fabulous Las Vegas."

Allegedly named by a police officer from Los Angeles after his hometown's Sunset Strip, The Strip is home to some of the world's largest hotels, casinos, and resorts. Most of The Strip is in the town of Paradise, Clark County. Only a small section of it is actually in the city of Las Vegas.

The first hotel to be built on The Strip was the 63-room El Rancho Vegas in 1941. Its success triggered a minor hotel-casino building boom in the 1940s. Early hotels included the Hotel Last

Frontier in 1942 and Thunderbird, Club Bingo, and The Flamingo in 1946. As these hotels were built, the area evolved to become The Strip.

It was The Flamingo that brought fame to the area. Built by mobster Benjamin "Bugsy" Siegel, a member of the Meyer Lansky crime organization, the hotel boasted giant pink neon signs. In 1968, Kirk Kerkorian purchased The Flamingo. In 1969, Kerkorian opened the International Hotel. With 1,512 rooms, it was the largest hotel in the world. It is now the Las Vegas Hilton. The MGM Grand Hotel and Casino opened in 1973. It was the biggest hotel-casino in the world until the Mirage, a mega-resort, opened in 1989.

Today, The Strip is synonymous with gambling, neon lights, and nightlife entertainment, and attracts many tourists from around the world.

HOW ARE CODES BROKEN?

Code breaking is a centuries-old art. Also known as cryptanalysis (from the Greek word *kryptos*, meaning "hidden"), it is used to decipher encrypted messages. This art is particularly important during wartime. Breaking the code of the Zimmermann telegram played a large role in the entry of the United States into World War I. As late as 2004, it was reported that the United States had broken Iranian codes.

As technology has improved throughout the years, methods of cryptanalysis have changed considerably. Originally done with pen and paper, cryptanalysis was later done using machines—most notably the Enigma in World War II—and is now usually done using computers.

Historically, the way to break codes was by frequency analysis, which some computer programs still employ. With simple codes, in which each letter (or word) is replaced with another letter (or a number), code breakers look for the most commonly occurring letter, and correspond it with the most common letters in normal language, such as *e* or *a*. Knowing certain pattern information about the code, such as "Dear Sir" at the start of a letter or "STOP" to end a sentence, can help with the frequency analysis and structure analysis of the document. Some educated guesswork can then play a part. As codes became more complex (the first highly complex codes were "two-part" codes with no predictable relationship between the text and the code), high-level mathematics are required to break them, including techniques such as integer factorization.

The advent of computers has meant that code-breaking techniques have become far more sophisticated, but so have the codes themselves. Many modern codes have yet to be broken, and other means, such as bugging and interception, must be used to discover information. However, some codes, such as those used with cell phones, can be easily broken with widely available computer programs.

WHAT IS THE DIFFERENCE BETWEEN A MUSHROOM AND A TOADSTOOL?

Mushrooms are edible fungi that are commonly eaten as a side order or used in sauces. The technical term for the spore-producing structure of mushrooms is the basidiocarp. Although mushrooms are a popular food, there is some confusion as to the difference between a mushroom and a toadstool, the latter being viewed with skepticism (and deservedly so).

In fact, there is no biological difference between a mushroom and a toadstool. But mushrooms are edible and toadstools are not.

There are thousands of different types of mushrooms and toadstools, so it can be difficult to distinguish one from the other. The distinction is important, however, as toadstools are generally poisonous.

There are a few ways to help determine whether a mushroom is "true" and edible. Edible mushrooms are often found growing in open fields or on lawns, unlike toadstools,

which tend to grow under shrubs or trees. The cap of the mushroom should be smooth and white, with no warts. Many dangerous toadstools have a rough and colorful cap. For example, the poisonous fly agaric toadstool is red with white spots.

The underside of the cap of a true mushroom tends to be covered with narrow gills that are pink or brown. The gills of toadstools are usually white. When the cap is removed, the gills of a true mushroom stay attached to the cap, whereas with a toadstool, they sometimes pull away with the stalk. The base of the stem of a toadstool also tends to be swollen, while the true mushroom's base is narrow or the same width as the rest of the stem.

Although there are many ways to differentiate between a mushroom and a toadstool, if there is any doubt, exercise extreme caution.

WHY DO ROOSTERS CROW?

To the bane of many country dwellers, roosters are often heard crowing in the early hours of the morning. The sound they make is generally written as *cock-a-doodle-do*. It is one of the commonest sounds of rural life. Many people believe that roosters crow as the sun rises as an announcement of the dawn of a new day. But roosters often crow before the sun rises. It is thought that they crow on a daily cycle, and the internal "body clock" of the rooster anticipates the dawn and wakes the rooster for crowing. If the rooster's body clock wakes him early, crowing will start before dawn.

Some believe that a rooster crows to attract hens, and because this may also attract predators, the safest time to crow is before the sun is very high in the sky. Others think a rooster crows to indicate that he has found some food that is worthy of note, or to keep the flock together if any chickens venture out of sight. Others believe that a rooster crows when it is in high spirits.

Most ornithologists now agree that the main purpose of the crow is to establish and mark out the rooster's territory. Before they were domesticated, roosters traveled with flocks of hens and would claim areas for their territory, warding off competing roosters with a powerful crow. The reason roosters tend to crow from a prominent vantage point, such as a fence post, is to make themselves clearly visible to their competitors and so that the noise travels farther. Ornithologists say that the reason most roosters crow early in the morning is because, like other birds, that is when they are most active. The morning is the start of a new day, and the rooster is crowing to reaffirm his territory to outsiders.

But roosters are known to crow at any time of the day or night. This may be prompted by a foreign noise that the rooster interprets as a challenge and so feels the need to announce his territory. Once one rooster starts crowing, it tends to stimulate others to follow suit. The most effective way to reduce or stop a rooster from crowing is castration. This procedure leaves the rooster with less of the male hormones and so less of an inclination to defend his territory.

HOW DO STEROIDS ENHANCE SPORTS PERFORMANCE?

Drugs in sport have been a hot topic for more than 25 years. In particular, the use of anabolic steroids is highly contentious, especially after the high-profile banning of Ben Johnson after he won the 1988 Olympic 100 meters athletics gold medal. The use of steroids in sport has recently received much publicity with the Lance Armstrong controversy.

Many athletes and medical professionals believe that the use of steroids enhances performance. Anabolic steroids are synthetic compounds whose structure is similar to the male sex hormone testosterone. This hormone has an anabolic effect on the body; that is, it increases the growth of muscular and skeletal tissue. It also has an androgenic effect, which results in an increase in male sexual characteristics. Anabolic steroids bind to hormone receptors and stimulate the synthesis of certain enzymes, which increase phosphocreatine synthesis and protein synthesis. Phosphocreatine synthesis allows athletes to train harder and longer, while protein synthesis helps to increase muscle mass. Steroids also stimulate bone marrow and increase the production of red blood cells. A large intake of protein by athletes is also essential to increase the muscle mass. Without the use of anabolic steroids, muscles build up slowly, but steroids reverse the short-term catabolic effect, promoting nitrogen retention, and this also helps build muscle mass quickly.

Apart from the increase in power from added muscle bulk, and the ability to train more, steroids can help to enhance performance in other ways. The increase in male hormones in the body increases aggression and motivation, which can positively affect training and performance. The use of steroids is also thought by some to have a positive psychological effect on performance.

Some experts claim that steroids do not enhance performance; a number of studies have been inconclusive on this point. Despite this difference of opinion, there is an array of incontrovertible side effects from anabolic steroid use. High blood pressure, stress, aggression, severe acne, and sexual dysfunction are some of them. In extreme cases, steroid use is thought to lead to brain cancer.

WHY DO CLOCKS WITH ROMAN NUMERALS USE *IIII* INSTEAD OF *IV*?

The Roman numeral for *4* is *IV*, yet clocks that use Roman numerals substitute *IIII* instead. A few theories have been put forward to explain this.

One theory is that *IV* represented the first two letters of the name of the god Jupiter, and to use *IV* for the number *4* was considered blasphemous. A more widespread view is that the Romans commonly used *IIII* instead of *IV* to avoid complicating things by requiring subtraction. Writing *4* as *IIII* instead of *IV* was more intuitive and appealed to those with limited reading skills or mathematics skills. It is thought that *IV* has become more commonly used only in modern times. In fact, manuscripts from the 1300s have been found that use both *IIII* and *IV*. Nowadays, clocks use *IIII* for *4* as well as *IX* for *9*, the latter requiring subtraction.

Many believe that *IIII* was used because it creates a visual symmetry with *VIII* on the other side of the clock face. The number *IV* is also difficult to read upside down or at an angle. Others say that early clockmakers needed only one mold to make the numbers if *IIII* was used, whereas using *IV* would have required an additional mold and more expense.

A further theory is that Louis XIV of France preferred *IIII* to *IV*. He ordered his clockmakers to use *IIII*, and the style has remained to this day.

WHAT DO THE NAUTICAL MEASUREMENTS *KNOT, FATHOM,* AND *LEAGUE* MEAN?

The knot, the fathom, and the league are commonly used nautical terms, yet their exact meanings are not widely known.

A knot is 1 nautical mile per hour, which is about 1.15 miles per hour on land. The origin of the term is the custom of casting a wooden log from a ship to measure the speed of the ship. The log was attached to the ship by a line of rope, which was divided by knots tied in the rope to help measure the ship's speed.

A fathom is 6 feet, or 183 centimeters. It comes from the Old English word *faedm*, meaning "outstretched arms." The distance between a pair of outstretched arms was the earliest definition of the length of a fathom. Originally used to measure land, it is now usually used only as a nautical measurement of depth.

A league is 3 statute miles, which is 5,280 yards (4,828 meters). It derives from the Latin word *leuga* meaning "a measure of distance." It is generally considered the distance that a horse or man can walk in an hour. It was used in ancient Rome, where it was also defined as 3 miles.

❓ WHAT ARE THE MOST COMMON METHODS OF TORTURE?

The concept of torture has existed for thousands of years. It has always been a common method of interrogation and is used by governments, police, terrorist organizations, and the Mafia.

In medieval times, torture was simple. Stretching the victim on the rack, whipping the victim, using fire on the victim, impaling the victim, and threatening the victim with wild animals were all common methods. Another was the strappado. It involved binding the victim's hands behind the back and suspending the victim, which would dislocate the arm joints. Thumbscrews and stocks were also used.

Technology has ushered in more sophisticated torture. A victim may be forced to eat chemicals or have chemicals inserted into various orifices, causing extreme pain and internal damage. Administering electrical shocks to the body is also common, as depicted in the 1987 movie *Lethal Weapon*.

Modern times have seen physical torture combined with psychological torture. Subjecting the victim to extended periods of solitary confinement and sleep deprivation is a method of torture, as is subjecting him or her to extremely high levels of noise to interfere with sleep and thought patterns. Depriving the victim of food is another technique, as is humiliating the victim by removing his or her clothes and forcing the victim to perform perverse acts. Verbally abusing a victim, threatening his or her family, and subjecting a victim to things that are contrary to his or her beliefs are also common. Forcing a victim to witness atrocities being inflicted on others is another technique.

Despite it being illegal under the Geneva Convention, it is thought that torture is still practiced today in more than half of the world's countries.

❓ WHAT IS THE ORIGIN OF KISSING UNDER THE MISTLETOE?

At Christmas, a sprig of the mistletoe plant is often used as decoration. Tradition has it that if a man and a woman find themselves together under the mistletoe, they should kiss.

The mistletoe has long been associated with folklore, and the history of kissing under it harks back to ancient Scandinavia, where it was said that if two enemies met under mistletoe in the forest, they would call a truce until the next morning. The tradition is also found in a Norse myth. The Norse goddess Frigga had a son called Baldur, whom she protected by making every animal, plant, and inanimate object promise not to harm him. However, Frigga overlooked the mistletoe, and Baldur was killed by a spear made from it. This brought winter to the world, and Frigga made the mistletoe sacred, ordering that it would also bring love into the world. This led to people kissing if they passed the plant together.

The mistletoe was also believed to make a person fertile and was associated with the Greek festival of Saturnalia. It was later used in marriage rites. It was also a sacred plant to the Celtic Druids, who, on the sixth night of the moon, would cut it with a golden sickle. Two white bulls would then be sacrificed, and prayers would be said to help the recipients of the mistletoe to prosper. In the Middle Ages, mistletoe was hung from ceilings to ward off evil spirits and witches.

The magic of the mistletoe continued into eighteenth-century England. A ball of mistletoe was used to decorate houses, and any girl standing beneath this decoration could not refuse a kiss. If a girl remained unkissed, legend had it that she would not marry in the next year.

The Christmas tradition of kissing under the mistletoe is observed today throughout most of the Western world.

HOW DID MOTHER'S DAY ORIGINATE?

Mother's Day is a day designated for people to thank their mothers and give them cards and gifts.

The concept of celebrating motherhood has existed since antiquity. Ancient Greeks worshipped Rhea, the mother of the gods, while the equivalent goddess in Rome, Cybele, was worshipped from as early as 250 BC. In the Middle Ages, young apprentices were said to be released to visit their families at a certain time of the year, that of Mothering Sunday.

The modern honoring of our own mothers started with Julia Ward Howe. A poet and social reformer, she wrote the "Battle Hymn of the Republic." In 1872, she suggested that a day be set aside that was dedicated to peace and to honoring mothers. In 1907, Anna Jarvis of Philadelphia helped to establish the official observance of Mother's Day. She campaigned for a holiday in remembrance of her own mother, who had arranged a Mothers Friendship Day picnic as a way to help heal the scars of the Civil War. In 1907, two years after her mother's death, Jarvis held a ceremony in Grafton, West Virginia. She then campaigned to create a formal holiday to honor mothers. By 1911, Mother's Day was celebrated by most US states, and in 1914, President Woodrow Wilson proclaimed Mother's Day a national holiday, to be held on the second Sunday in May.

Mother's Day is now celebrated throughout most of the Western world, although it occurs at different times of the year in different countries. Many still observe it on the second Sunday in May, although in the United Kingdom it falls on the fourth Sunday in Lent, which is usually in March or April.

 HOW ARE SWORDS SWALLOWED?

Sword swallowing is an extremely dangerous performance art. It is considered something of a lost art, with fewer than 50 performers existing in the world today.

Sword swallowing originated in India around 2000 BC as a demonstration of divine power. It wasn't until the AD ninth century in China that it was used to amuse people. Throughout the Middle Ages, it was done by street performers. Later, it was performed in the United States in circuses.

Sword swallowing involves inserting a sword into the mouth and down the esophagus, all the way to the stomach. The gag reflex must be suppressed, and the performer must avoid actually swallowing for the entire time the sword is inserted. The most effective technique is to completely relax the throat. It is also recommended to use a sword with blunt sides, so that the sword does not cut the throat on the way down. The sword should also not be too long, to prevent puncturing the bottom of the stomach. The sword should be clean, so that no dust or other foreign matter can irritate the throat. The performer must also be careful to avoid the breastbone while the sword is being inserted.

Over the years, the practice of sword swallowing has resulted in many serious injuries and deaths.

WHAT DOES IT MEAN WHEN A PERSON "GIVES YOU A WHITE ELEPHANT"?

A person who gives you a white elephant has given you something that is more trouble than it is worth.

A white, or albino, elephant is a rare kind of elephant. In ancient times in Asia, and in particular, Thailand, white elephants were regarded as sacred. Even in modern times, the white elephant is considered a symbol of royal power, and any found are presented to the king of Thailand. The more white elephants that the king has, the more powerful he is perceived to be. The present king of Thailand, Bhumibol Adulyadej, has 10 white elephants.

To keep a white elephant in captivity is an expensive task, which only the rich can afford. The elephants have special dietary requirements and must be accessible to people for worship. Lower-grade white elephants were sometimes gifted by the Thai king to enemies or people with whom the king was dissatisfied. The elephants were sacred, so they could not be put to work. Obliged to care for the animal, the financial burden could ruin the recipient. This scenario gave rise to the expression.

WHAT CAUSES "THE BENDS" IN SOME SCUBA DIVERS?

Decompression sickness (DCS) is a potentially lethal condition that occurs when moving from a high-pressure environment to a low-pressure environment too quickly. First recorded in 1841, it is common in deep-sea divers, who can experience rashes; pain in the head, neck, and torso; breathing difficulties; or nervous system problems, such as weakness, numbness, or shooting pains on one side of the body. Another symptom is "the bends," or pains in the joints of the arms and legs and an inability to bend them. Although DCS is often called the bends, this set of symptoms is only one aspect of DCS.

Divers breathe pressurized air, which is mostly nitrogen, from tanks. In the high pressure under the ocean, the nitrogen is absorbed by the body's fatty tissues rather than being breathed out. The deeper a diver goes, the higher the pressure of the nitrogen and the more that is absorbed. This nitrogen is not utilized by the body and instead is stored. If a diver rises too quickly and the pressure of the nitrogen in the body drops rapidly, the nitrogen turns from liquid to bubbles, in the manner of a shaken can of soda. The nitrogen bubbles out of the blood and tissues uncontrollably, causing blockages of blood flow and damage to various parts of the body, particularly the lungs, heart, and brain. Nitrogen is also stored in the joints (which creates the bends) and just under the skin (which causes a rash).

To avoid DCS, a diver must rise slowly or make intermittent stops on the way up, so that the nitrogen can be released from the tissues gradually and not bubble out. Once symptoms develop, entering a decompression chamber can also help, by matching the previous high pressure and allowing the nitrogen to release slowly as the pressure is decreased.

Most DCS symptoms appear within an hour of surfacing, and nearly all appear within six hours. The damage sustained can be permanent.

WHAT ARE THE FASTEST LAND, WATER, AND AIR ANIMALS?

People are often fascinated with the largest, strongest, and most dangerous animals. Which is the fastest animal is also of great interest. To answer the question properly, the fastest animals in the three different mediums—land, water, and air—need to be considered.

The fastest land animal is the cheetah. Over short distances, it can reach speeds of up to 70 miles per hour. Found in Africa, it is a cat built for speed. Virtually every part of its body is adapted to maximize its velocity. Large nostrils and lungs provide for quick air intake, nonretractable claws provide traction, and a streamlined body cuts through the air. Its lithe spine and bone structure, including small collarbones, increase the length of its stride, and its large hind legs and heart greatly assist its speed.

In the water, fish dominate. Although measuring the speed of fish is difficult, the fastest is thought to be the Indo-Pacific (or cosmopolitan) sailfish. It grows up to 220 pounds and has been recorded at speeds of up to 68 miles per hour, similar to the cheetah on land. It feeds on schooling fish, such as sardines and anchovies. At full tilt, its fins are completely folded back against its body to minimize its width. Other fast fish include the swordfish (56 miles per hour) and the tuna (44 miles per hour).

The fastest bird (and in fact the fastest animal) is the peregrine falcon. Its cruising speed is up to 68 miles per hour. And its diving speed has been recorded at up to 273 miles per hour. It possesses a short, slim tail and tapered wings. It feeds on smaller birds and lizards, capturing prey with its talons and killing with its beak.

WHAT IS THE DIFFERENCE BETWEEN "PARTLY SUNNY" AND "PARTLY CLOUDY" IN A WEATHER REPORT?

A frequently asked question of meteorologists is the difference between "partly sunny" and "partly cloudy." Taking the words at face value, there seems to be no difference between the two.

Although a number of meteorologists admit that use of the terms involves a degree of subjectivity on the part of the forecaster, it is generally accepted that one of these forecasts will be given if there is cloud cover for between 30 and 70 percent of the day. Some forecasters explain that the choice of term has a lot to do with the weather over the prior few days and that psychology plays a role. If the weather has been wet but looks as though it is clearing up, the forecast will often be partly sunny, because it sounds more positive. However, if sunny weather has prevailed but it is now turning gray, it will usually be partly cloudy.

Others say that because there is little difference between the two, "partly sunny" will be used during the day, when the sun is visible, whereas "partly cloudy" will be used at night, when the sun is down anyway.

Some meteorologists claim that there is more science to it, and that a 30 to 50 percent covering of cloud means "partly cloudy," whereas a 50 to 70 percent covering means "partly sunny." In this definition, "partly cloudy" means either an equal amount of sun and cloud or slightly more sun than cloud, and "partly sunny" means either an equal amount of cloud and sun or slightly more cloud than sun.

Despite the different explanations, some meteorologists admit that the two terms essentially mean the same thing and that they exist alongside each other solely to give the forecaster a wider vocabulary.

CAN HOLDING IN A FART KILL YOU?

Flatulence, colloquially known as farting, is considered taboo in most social settings, particularly if accompanied by an unpleasant odor or noise. This unacceptability makes many feel compelled to hold in any gas. This has led some to ask whether this retention of flatulence is harmful.

For centuries, it has been believed that retaining flatulence could be dangerous. The Roman emperor Claudius even passed a law legalizing flatulence at banquets because of health concerns. At the time, the widespread opinion was that a person could be poisoned if gas was not emitted immediately.

Flatulence is a mixture of gases that are produced by bacteria and yeasts in the intestinal tract and released through the anus. Most animals and all mammals flatulate, with the average person releasing up to a third of a gallon of gas per day. The gas consists primarily of oxygen, nitrogen, carbon dioxide, hydrogen, and methane. The presence of sulfuric components is responsible for the common odor.

These gases that constitute flatulence are not harmful to human health and are a natural aspect of the intestinal contents. They are not in any way poisonous, and no particular harm can result from holding in flatulence. The main side effect of this retentive practice is the discomfort of a stomachache from the buildup of gas pressure in the intestines. Some medical professionals claim that in extreme circumstances, the practice can result in a distension of the bowel, potentially leading to constipation.

HOW DO MARTIAL ARTISTS BREAK THINGS WITH THEIR BARE HANDS?

For years, martial artists have demonstrated their ability to break multiple bricks or planks of wood by striking the dense objects with their bare hands. This seemingly superhuman ability has led some to question whether a trick or illusion is involved. In fact, the seemingly supernatural skill is mastered purely by training and technique.

Martial arts students are trained to break small objects early on in their careers. As they practice for long periods, they create tiny fractures in the bones of the hands, which heal with additional calcium deposits. This enlarges and strengthens the hands, making them more able to break larger objects, and reducing the chance of injury.

It is the amount of force that is applied that breaks the object. To create force, the artist must create as much hand speed as possible. The greater the speed of the hand, the more likely that the break will be successful. Studies show that maximum hand speed is achieved when the arm is about 80 percent extended. One of the main techniques used to hit the object at this maximum speed is to focus beyond the object, as if you were trying to hit a few inches beyond it. This ensures that the hand does not decelerate prior to contact with the target. To ensure high speed, it is also important to relax, as tension can make the body stiffen and so produce less speed. Some say the hand should be pulled back quickly after the strike, which provides a faster, whippier technique, like a snake biting.

Although immense skill and technique are involved, the boards or bricks are usually not stacked together but are separated by pencils. This means that they are broken one at a time, instead of as a block. The boards are also struck parallel to the grain, so that they are easier to break.

WHY DO FAST-MOVING WHEELS APPEAR TO GO BACKWARD ON FILM?

Often in movies and on television, the spoked wheels of a vehicle appear to rotate backward. This is known as the reverse rotation effect, or the wagon-wheel effect, because it was originally noticed with the spokes of wagon wheels.

It is actually an optical illusion, caused by an intermittent display or recording system. Movie and television cameras generally operate at between 24 and 30 frames per second— that is, they flash on and off that many times per second. Because of the speed, the eyes can't see the separate film frames, and the brain perceives the film as continuous. If the spokes of a wheel rotate at a multiple of the same number of frames per second, they appear to be in the same exact position every time the shutter opens. This makes them seem motionless. However, if the wheel slows down slightly, the spokes of the wheel do not have time to rotate to the same position before the shutter opens again. Consequently, the spokes of the wheel appear to be rotating backward.

This same effect can be seen in films of helicopter rotors and aircraft propellers, and can also occur if lighting is temporally modulated, such as with strobe lighting. When

an alternating current is used, light flickers at an increased rate and can cause the same effect. But some studies report that people can see the reverse rotation effect with a wheel illuminated by continuous light in real conditions. This has led to a theory that, as with a movie, human vision is a series of still frames, which are perceived to be continuous. These studies suggest that this effect is generally seen in real life only after prolonged gazing.

WHY DO DOGS SNIFF EACH OTHER'S BEHINDS?

Much to the embarrassment of their owners, when dogs meet, they typically sniff each other's behinds.

Dogs engage in this seemingly perverse activity because the area around the tail provides a great deal of distinguishing information. Chemical substances are produced by dogs and secreted by special anal glands or in their urine. In sniffing around the tail, a dog uses its extremely acute sense of smell to determine another dog's identity, physiology, and emotions.

While dogs sniff each other, they also adopt certain postures, such as tensing the body and holding the ears back. The dogs are gathering information to determine which one is dominant, whether the other dog is friendly, and whether the other dog has been spayed or neutered. Once these factors are determined, the dogs usually relax.

This instinctive ritual is an important procedure for dogs; they should not be dissuaded from sniffing each other.

WHAT ARE THE ORIGINS OF MALE CIRCUMCISION?

Male circumcision has been practiced for centuries. The first evidence of it comes from ancient Egypt, where tomb artwork from as early as 2300 BC depicts men with circumcised penises. Some Egyptian mummies have also been found to be circumcised.

Circumcision was common among Semitic people in 600 BC and, although different views were held, many Jews and Christians were circumcised in the AD first century. However, many European Christians did not practice it until the 1700s.

It is not known exactly why circumcision began. Many believe it was initially practiced as a religious sacrifice or rite of passage into adulthood. This was particularly so for the Jews. Other theories propose that it was done to reduce masturbation, which was considered a cause of various diseases. This is said to be a main reason for it in the late 1800s. It was also common during Queen Victoria's reign as a mark of high social status. Many male members of the royal family were circumcised during this period. It was also often carried out for hygienic purposes when frequent bathing was not usual.

Circumcision was widely practiced in many Western countries in the twentieth century until a 1971 American medical report stated that there is no valid medical reason for it. Since then, the incidence of circumcision has declined greatly, although it is still practiced today.

WHAT ARE THE PRINCIPLES OF FENG SHUI?

Feng shui is the art of placing objects and arranging space in a way that is harmonious with the environment. Literally meaning "wind water," the practice originated in China thousands of years ago and was introduced to the United States by Chinese immigrants in the 1800s.

The basis of feng shui is the notion of living in balance with nature, so that both people and the environment benefit. Feng shui claims that our lives are affected by our environments and that to be happy we need to surround ourselves with symbols of beauty and kindness.

Traditional Chinese feng shui uses a special compass called a *luopan* to design and map out cities, buildings, and grave sites. Complex mathematical equations are employed in this extremely technical discipline, as are core theories, texts, and methods.

Modern feng shui is much less ambitious and simpler. Feng shui methods are coupled with architecture and interior design to arrange a home and the objects in it to obtain an optimal flow of energy. Examples of considerations are which directions doorways should face, where mirrors should hang, and where the heads of beds should be. A feng shui master, who makes decisions based on the flow of energy in an environment and on where certain electromagnetic fields are located, can determine these things.

❓ WHAT DOES TRAINSPOTTING INVOLVE?

Trainspotting is a hobby of railroad enthusiasts. Known in the United States as railfans or railbuffs, trainspotters are very common in Europe and the United Kingdom. A railfan's interests often extend to all aspects of railway systems, including engines, lines, stations, systems, and equipment. Trainspotting is a narrower field, with the trainspotter concentrating on watching and tracking the trains that pass.

The goal of many trainspotters is to try to see every piece of rolling stock for a particular railway company. To do this, they often collect detailed information about the movements of particular trains. To assist them, trainspotters usually carry books containing a list of trains for a company, as well as a notebook to check off the trains that they have seen. Some trainspotters use tape recorders or cameras to monitor their findings. Websites also exist to allow an exchange of information. Trainspotters often congregate at particular stations, such as junction stations, through which a large number of trains pass.

The British Transport Police utilize the vast knowledge of trainspotters, who commonly report vandalism or suspicious circumstances. Trainspotters are also known to provide information on malfunctioning equipment to the rail companies.

It is thought that trainspotters are motivated by the appeal of train nostalgia or the power of such large machines. Bashers have evolved from trainspotters; the goal of these rail aficionados is to ride on every train possible.

WHAT CAUSES PREMENSTRUAL SYNDROME?

Premenstrual syndrome (PMS) is the stress that some women experience prior to menstruation. It normally occurs in the week leading up to menstruation, and its symptoms include cramping, bloating, depression, irritability, and anxiety.

Although PMS is thought to occur in up to 75 percent of women who menstruate, scientists are not exactly sure what causes it. Many scientists believe it is a response to an imbalance of female hormones during the menstrual cycle. This leads to a buildup of salt and water in the system, as well as a decrease in the hormone progesterone. An imbalance of progesterone can reduce the levels of serotonin in the brain, a chemical that helps control moods. A woman's diet is also thought to play a role in PMS. But some studies have found that placebo drugs (fake drugs, which have no effect) have reduced the symptoms of PMS as much as actual drugs. This has led a number of people to controversially suggest that PMS is a socially constructed or psychological condition.

Vitamin supplements, such as vitamin B6, as well as exercise, have been shown to reduce symptoms, as has reducing the intake of caffeine, alcohol, sugar, and sodium. Herbal remedies, such as evening primrose oil, are also thought to help by their stimulation of the pituitary gland, which regulates the hormones estrogen and progesterone.

❓ WHAT CAUSES "SEXUAL CHEMISTRY" BETWEEN TWO PEOPLE?

Sometimes two people experience an instant attraction. The reason for this attraction might be unclear, and they might chalk it up to "sexual chemistry." But what causes sexual chemistry?

A large factor in sexual attraction is physical appearance. If two people find each other visually attractive, there will likely be a certain amount of "chemistry." If the people's personalities then also match well, this normally increases the attraction. In addition to these factors, it is now believed that pheromones play a major role in sexual chemistry.

Pheromones are chemical substances that many animals secrete in order to attract mates. A special organ in the nasal cavity generally detects them. Pheromones can produce a profound effect on some animals, often promoting instant attraction. Studies in recent years have shown that, like other animals, humans also produce odorless pheromones, which waft into the air. It is also likely that people can detect pheromones and subconsciously be influenced by them. If a person finds the chemicals of the pheromone appealing, he or she is more likely to be attracted to the person who has emitted them, and an otherwise inexplicable sexual chemistry will result.

Although the study of human pheromones is a young science, cosmetic companies have produced perfumes that supposedly contain pheromones that are irresistible to the opposite sex. One such cologne for men contains androstenol, an alleged pheromone made from sweat and tears. There is no evidence to suggest that these fragrances are successful.

WHY DOES TOUCHING METAL SOMETIMES CAUSE AN ELECTRICAL SHOCK?

On a cold winter's day, you might experience an electrical shock upon touching a piece of metal. This type of shock is due to static electricity.

When two different insulating surfaces are touched together, opposite charges within the two surfaces are separated. Walking on a rug while wearing shoes is often enough to separate the negative from the positive charges, creating a surface charge imbalance on your shoes and in your body—the shoes pick up additional negative charges and leave positive ones behind, creating the imbalance. This rubbing of two nonconductive objects against each other generates static electricity, which you feel when you touch a metal object. This often occurs when a car door is opened.

Static electricity is more prevalent in environments with little humidity. This is why more electrical shocks are felt during winter, when humidity is less. There are a number of items that, when rubbed together, typically create static electricity, but common ones are shoes rubbing against a floor or clothes rubbing against skin.

You can reduce the number of electrical shocks you receive. Increasing the humidity in the air is one way. Or ground yourself: Touch the metal with something else, such as car keys, which will receive the shock instead. Dry skin is also more susceptible to accumulating the electrical charges, so using moisturizer can minimize the shocks.

WHY DO PEOPLE'S EYES SOMETIMES APPEAR RED IN PHOTOGRAPHS?

Much to the chagrin of photographers, when a photo is taken with a flash at night, the eyes of the subject of the photo might appear bright red.

This is the red-eye effect. It happens because the light of the flash occurs too fast for the iris (the colored part of the eye) to close the pupil. As a result, the flash is focused by the lens of the eye on the retina at the back of the eye. The retina is covered with tiny blood vessels, and these red vessels are focused by the lens of the eye back to the camera. This makes the eyes in the photograph appear red.

The more open the pupils are, the greater the red-eye effect, as the more the illuminated retina can be seen. The effect is also generally more pronounced in people with light eye color and also in children, whose eyes tend to be lighter. This is because pale irises have less melanin in them and allow more light to pass through to the retina.

The red-eye effect also occurs in many animals, such as cats, which have a light-reflecting layer behind the retina that acts to improve night vision. This layer also increases the red-eye effect, although the color varies from animal to animal.

The red-eye effect can be reduced by using a bounce flash, which is aimed at a nearby wall and so enters the eye at a different angle, or by using a special camera that employs a series of low-level flashes before the main flash. This allows the iris to contract to reduce the effect. Increasing the lighting in a room so that the pupils are not as open also reduces the effect.

IS THERE ANY SCIENCE TO PALM READING?

Palm reading is an art used by fortune-tellers to perceive the character, fortune, and future of a person by studying that individual's palm. It is also known as chiromancy (from the Greek words *kheir* meaning "hand" and *manteia* meaning "divination") and derives originally from Greek mythology.

People's hands are like fingerprints: no two are identical. A fortune-teller "reads" a person's palm by interpreting the different "lines" and "mounts" on the hand, which supposedly reveal things about him or her.

There are three main lines on the hand. The heart line is the top line across the hand. It indicates a person's emotional feelings, such as depression or happiness, as well as a person's romantic situation and the physical well-being of his or her heart. The head line is the next line down, and it runs across the middle of the palm. This line represents a person's intelligence, creativity, and communication style. The life line is the next major line. It arcs from the left of the palm and down to the wrist. This line indicates a person's health

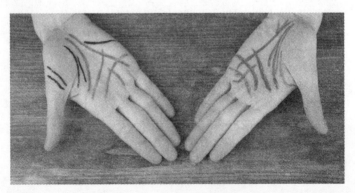

and general well-being. It is also said to indicate any major life changes, although, contrary to popular belief, its length is unrelated to the length of a person's life.

There are other lines, including the simian crease, the fate line, and the sun, union, Mercury, and travel lines. These are said to indicate an array of things, from business acumen to fame and whether a person is going to travel long distances.

Although fortune-tellers swear that their readings are accurate, fortune-telling is classed by many as a pseudoscience, lacking any scientific evidentiary substance.

CAN A PERSON BE FROZEN AND THEN BROUGHT BACK TO LIFE?

Science fiction films often portray people who have been frozen and then restored to life. Although this scenario is considered by many to be fanciful, with advances in modern technology it just might become possible.

Cryonics is the preservation of bodies at extremely low temperatures. Although bacteria and even small animals, such as frogs, can be frozen and then returned to a living state when thawed, larger animals, such as humans, cannot. This is because the freezing process of removing heat through thick tissue is too slow, and ice crystals grow and damage the body's cells irreparably. But using cryoprotectants, which allow water to vitrify rather than freeze, prevents ice crystals from forming. Vitrification does not freeze tissue but preserves it in a glassy state. This prevents the molecules from rearranging themselves.

Some scientists believe a body vitrified using cryoprotectants can remain physically viable for thirty thousand years without damage to the structure of the brain. Although today's technology does not allow a frozen person to be revived, some believe that in the future—as medical technology improves—it could become a reality.

Although the practice is viewed with skepticism by most medical professionals, some scientists ardently believe in it. Cryonicists claim that even though a person is dead, if he or she is vitrified immediately after death, the person's organs will remain viable, just as a heart to be transplanted comes from a person who is dead but whose heart still beats.

A number of people have undergone this process in the hope that future technology will allow them to be revived, but the procedure and continued storage of the body are far too expensive for most people to afford. Only time will tell if the expense is worth it.

WHY DO BRITISH PUBS HAVE COLORFUL NAMES?

Many pubs in the UK have striking names. What is the history behind this?

The naming of pubs dates back to the AD twelfth century. Many pubs were originally built in this time, and most patrons in this era were illiterate. As words could not be read, pictorial signs were used, so that a pub could be recognized and people could refer to it. For example, a pub with a painting of a cat and a fiddle could become known as the Cat and Fiddle.

This practice began by pub owners placing an object in front of their establishments. Names from this time include the Boot and the Copper Kettle.

Once painted signs began to be used, a wider array of names was possible. These were derived from many areas. Royalty and heraldry was a popular naming base. The Red Lion, for example, dates back to the 1600s, when James I and VI of Scotland came to the throne and the red lion of Scotland  was used as a royal symbol. The White Boar came from the emblem of Richard III. Historical events also provided names, such as The Trafalgar and The Royal Oak, as did personal titles, such as The Prince of Wales. Animals, myths and legends, and sports and pastimes were also used. The Fox and Hounds is a common name.

Today, most pubs in the United Kingdom are named using this interesting style.

HOW DOES DNA IDENTIFICATION WORK?

DNA is an abbreviation of deoxyribonucleic acid, an acid that is found in cells and that contains the genetic building blocks for all forms of life. It is made up of genes from both parents. Although any two people have the majority of their DNA sequence in common, they also have variable repeating sequences, known as microsatellites, which can be used to distinguish between people with an extremely high degree of certainty—the chance of error is around 1 in 100 billion.

Sir Alec Jeffreys invented DNA testing in 1985. It was first used in the Enderby murders case in Leicestershire, England, in 1986. Since then, DNA testing has been used extensively in forensic science to solve past and present crimes. It is also used in other areas, such as identifying dead bodies and paternity testing.

To carry out the testing, DNA is extracted from cells in a sample of blood, saliva, semen, hair, or tissue. A restriction enzyme is then used to cut the DNA into fragments, which are then separated into bands. The bands are transferred to a nylon membrane and treated with a radioactive probe, which binds to particular sequences on the membrane. An X-ray film is then used to detect the radioactive pattern and make a visible pattern of bands. This is the DNA "fingerprint," which can be distinguished from the DNA fingerprint of any other person.

 HOW DO FISH BREATHE?

Although whales and dolphins have lungs that store air, which they breathe from the surface, fish don't have lungs. Instead, they have evolved to breathe underwater.

Water contains a small percentage of dissolved oxygen. Fish use their gills to concentrate the oxygen and absorb it. Water flows into the fish's mouth and through the gills. The oxygen in the water passes into the blood-enriched gill structures called filaments and lamellae. The latter are thin, disk-shaped membranes that are filled with a dense capillary network. As the oxygen is absorbed, the carbon dioxide in the fish's bloodstream passes into the water and is removed from the body. There is essentially an exchange of oxygen and carbon dioxide across the capillary membrane. As water is pumped in and out of a fish's mouth, the fish is, in effect, breathing.

The gills have a large surface area to aid in the absorption of the oxygen. But the gills need to be immersed in water to support their weight. If a fish is on land, the gills collapse and the filaments stick to one another. Very little surface area is exposed to absorb oxygen, and this leads to a fish out of water lacking the oxygen it needs and consequently suffocating.

? WHAT CAUSES ALTITUDE SICKNESS?

Altitude sickness is a condition caused by a person's lack of adaptation to the difference in the atmosphere at high altitudes. It commonly occurs above 8,000 feet, and its symptoms include fatigue, shortness of breath, headaches, nausea, dizziness, loss of appetite, insomnia, and sometimes coma or death.

Although the proportion of oxygen in the air at higher altitudes remains the same as at lower altitudes, the pressure is lower and so the amount of oxygen available to the body is less. The number of oxygen molecules per breath is reduced, so the body must work harder to get the oxygen it needs. To compensate, a person will breathe harder. In addition, high altitudes and low pressure can cause fluid to leak from the capillaries in the lungs and brain, which can lead to fluid buildup and sickness.

The main cause of altitude sickness is going too high, too quickly. A person will acclimatize to high altitudes with time. It usually takes the body one to three days to acclimatize to a given altitude. After two days or so, the body produces more red blood cells to carry oxygen, and the pressure in pulmonary capillaries increases, forcing blood into parts of the lungs not normally used for breathing. The body also produces more of a particular enzyme that releases oxygen from hemoglobin to the body's tissues. The rule of thumb is to climb high during the day but return to a lower altitude to sleep, so that a person sleeps no more than 1,000 feet (300 meters) higher than the night before. By following this rule, a person can gradually sleep higher each night.

Different people have different susceptibilities to altitude sickness. Those with a diet high in carbohydrates tend to feel less sick because carbohydrates liberate more energy and oxygen. Drinking plenty of water also helps a person acclimatize by replacing fluids lost through heavy breathing. Ascending slowly and using oxygen chambers and pressure bags can also help. But the only genuine cure for altitude sickness is to return to a lower altitude.

WHAT IS THE ORIGIN OF "FREEZE THE BALLS OFF A BRASS MONKEY"?

To say that spending time outdoors would "freeze the balls off a brass monkey" means that the weather is very cold. But confusion exists about the origin of the expression.

Many believe the phrase originated in the British navy during the Napoleonic wars. It is alleged that cannonballs were placed on two brass plates, which was called a monkey. In cold weather, the balls and the brass monkey would shrink, and the balls would fall through the plates and on to the ship's deck. This is incorrect. The navy asserts that there is no evidence for this reputed origin. It is thought that brass was too expensive to use to hold cannonballs, and that cannonballs were kept on deck only during a battle and not otherwise. It is also thought that the contraction of the metals would not be sufficient for the balls to fall through.

The actual origin of the expression is unknown. Expressions about brass monkeys in the 1800s do not refer to balls but instead declare that it is cold enough to freeze the tail, nose, or ears off a brass monkey. They also say that it is hot enough to scald the throat or singe the hair off a brass monkey. An early recorded reference to a brass monkey is found in C. A. Abbey's 1857 book *Before the Mast*: "It would freeze the tail off a brass monkey." Kate Douglas Wiggin's *The Story of Waitstill Baxter* in 1913 mentions "talking the tail off a brass monkey." Talbot Mundy's 1919 work *The Ivory Trail* mentions "the gall of a brass monkey." In fact, many early references to the expression mention heat rather than cold. Herman Melville, in

his 1847 work *Omoo*, says that it is hot enough to "melt the nose off a brass monkey."

So although the exact origin of the phrase is unknown, it is likely that it had nothing to do with cannonballs on battleships.

WHY DOES THE POPE CHANGE HIS NAME?

When a new pope is elected and accepts his role, he traditionally selects a new name. This tradition dates back to 533, when Pope John II's name was changed from Mercurius. This name is derived from Mercury, a Roman god. Not wanting to use a name belonging to a pagan religion, he changed his name to honor a former pope.

Although some later popes retained their original name, it became the custom for a new name to be selected, which represents the new life that the pope is entering. The new name is often the name of the pope's favorite saint or a former pope whom the new pope admires. Sometimes the name of a family member is used, as with Pope John XXIII.

After the pope is elected, the dean of the College of Cardinals asks the successful cardinal, "Do you freely accept your election?" If the cardinal replies in the affirmative, he becomes pope at that instant. The dean then asks, "By what name shall you be called?" The pope then announces the name he has chosen. Although popes are permitted to use their birth name, to do so is very uncommon. The most recent pope to retain his birth name was Pope Marcellus II, who was pope in the year 1555.

The practice of selecting a new reign name has existed for thousands of years. In medieval times, monarchs frequently chose a different name when they ascended to the throne. Even ancient rulers did this, including Egyptian pharaohs, who usually went by a number of different names.

IS THE HUMAN BODY REALLY 80 PERCENT WATER?

It is often stated in health magazines that 80 percent of the human body is water. But is this actually true?

The human body depends on water. The amount of fluids in the body strongly influences a person's well-being. Although the exact percentage of water varies, depending on what source is quoted, scientists believe that we are in fact made up of around 72 percent water and 8 percent chemical compounds. The remaining 20 percent is bone and solid tissue. The water actually contains sodium chloride (salt) and potassium chloride, and about two-thirds of it is in our cells. The rest is free-flowing liquid in the form of blood plasma and liquid between the cells.

Water plays a vital role in maintaining all of the body's systems and also in repairing any damage to the body. Blood is more than 83 percent water, and in order for it to properly carry out its life-preserving functions, the body must be sufficiently hydrated. The brain, which controls every aspect of the body, is more than 80 percent water. The fluid inside the nerves is also made up of water and minerals.

Water also has a large impact on energy. The liver uses water to metabolize fat into usable energy. Drinking a lot of water speeds up the metabolism and results in increased strength and energy. A drop of 5 percent in body fluids causes a 30 percent drop in energy, and a 15 percent drop in body fluids causes death. Water is also important in keeping the temperature of the body constant.

Because so much of the body is water, it is advisable to drink a large amount of high-quality water to stay healthy. About 2 liters per day is recommended, depending on factors such as the ambient temperature and humidity and a person's level of activity.

❓ HOW AND WHY DO CRICKETS MAKE SUCH A LOUD NOISE?

Crickets are known for the loud chirping they make during the night. In fact, it is only the male cricket who chirps. But how and why does he do it so loudly?

The cricket is related to the grasshopper but has a flattened body. The male has special ridges on its wings, which rub against each other, like a comb against a file. There is a tiny row of teeth beneath the top wing and a scraper on the bottom wing. The edge of the scraper curves to fit between the teeth. The cricket rubs the two together extremely quickly—as fast as 4,000 teeth per second—and this produces the noise. The noise gets louder as it vibrates across the wing and into the air.

The male cricket has two types of song. The calling

song is particularly loud and is used to attract females and repel rival males. Females will travel great distances when a male is calling. Once the female is in close proximity to the male, the courting song becomes very quiet. The cricket is a nocturnal creature to help it evade the predators that are also attracted by its loud song.

The chirping of a cricket can last for hours and exceed 100 decibels. When a cricket is chirping at this volume, the nerve that transmits the sound to the cricket's brain is temporarily suppressed. This prevents the cricket from hearing his own deafening call, but he is still able to hear the calls of other crickets.

There are around 900 species of cricket, and in some countries they are eaten. In other countries, they are popular pets. In Asia, they are considered good luck.

❓ WHAT ARE SHOOTING STARS?

Shooting stars are frequently seen streaking across the sky. But what are they really?

A shooting star is actually a meteor. An extremely bright meteor is sometimes known as a fireball or bolide. A meteor is the visible path of a meteoroid, which is a small, solid piece of rock or dust entering Earth's atmosphere. This particle strikes the atmosphere at such a rate that it burns up and glows to produce a trail of light known as a shooting or falling star. Most meteors glow for only a few seconds, and that is what we see.

Most meteoroids are the size of a pebble and can travel up to 42 kilometers per second. As Earth moves around the sun, it runs into some of these small rocks that collide with Earth's atmosphere. A comet often leaves a trail of debris as it orbits the sun. When Earth passes through such a trail of debris, a meteor shower occurs.

If any part of the meteoroid passes through the atmosphere without burning up and hits Earth, it is known as a meteorite. More than 100 meteorites hit Earth every year, most of them very small. Some have been identified as moon rock and others as pieces of Mars. In 1902, an iron meteorite weighing 15 tons was found in Oregon that was believed to have landed thousands of years earlier.

WHY IS THE EMPIRE STATE BUILDING FAMOUS?

The Empire State Building in New York City is one of the most famous buildings in the world. It is a 102-story building that was built in 1931. In 1955, the American Society of Civil Engineers named the building one of the Seven Wonders of the Western Hemisphere, and it was also named the eighth modern wonder.

The fame of the building began during construction, when its completion date was hurried so that it could take the title of the world's tallest building from the Chrysler Building. Standing 1,455 feet high after a broadcasting tower was added in 1950, it remained the tallest building in the world until the World Trade Center was built. Following the September 11, 2001, terrorist strikes, it then became the tallest building in New York City, and the second tallest in the United States. Floodlights illuminate the top of the building at night with an array of seasonal or topical colors.

The workforce used to build the Empire State Building amounted to 3,400 during peak periods, and its famous art deco spire is visible throughout much of New York City. Its construction during the Great Depression at a cost of more than $24 million also helped to make it a monument to the city. Broadcasting began at the building in the 1930s, and it has been described as the most valuable building in American broadcasting, for both radio and television. The building has appeared in more than 90 movies, and was immortalized in *King Kong* in 1933. Other incidents have added to the building's notoriety. In 1945, at the end of World War II, an Army Air Corps bomber plane accidentally crashed into the seventy-ninth floor, killing 14 people. The building also has been used as the official welcoming landmark for distinguished foreign visitors, including Prince Charles, Queen Elizabeth II, and Fidel Castro.

With a public observatory gallery near the top of the building offering incredible views of the city, it is one of the most widely visited tourist attractions in America, receiving in excess of 4.3 million visitors every year.

❓ HOW DO SQUIRRELS FIND THEIR BURIED NUTS?

Squirrels are often seen either hiding nuts or digging them up to eat. They bury nuts so that they have food during the lean winter months. With the nuts so small and the areas in which they are buried so large, people sometimes question just how the squirrels find the nuts.

Scientists believe that squirrels possess an excellent spatial memory and make a mental map of where they bury their nuts. They also remember particular landmarks and different aspects of the environment to help them find the nuts.

The squirrel uses another cunning technique to find nuts. Before burying them, the squirrel will break the shell of the nut with its teeth and then clean the nut by rubbing it on

its face or licking it. This applies the squirrel's scent to the nut. Using its acute sense of smell, the squirrel is then able to locate the nut, even when it is covered by thick snow.

Of course, many nuts are never found, and this provides a good source of future trees.

? WHY DO PEOPLE HAVE FINGERPRINTS?

Fingerprints are the patterns on the skin of a finger. Fingerprints are unique and no two people, not even identical twins, have been found with the same set of fingerprints. Even primates have unique fingerprints, and it has been suggested that the fingerprints of cloned animals would also vary.

A person's fingerprints develop before birth and are affected by the environment in the womb. And they do not change with age. If a person's finger is damaged, it will heal so as to restore the original fingerprint.

Although it is not known why fingerprints are unique, scientists believe that their purpose is to help the grip. The whirls and ridges of the print provide traction for grasping objects. A smooth finger would have difficulty holding objects, which would be more likely to slip. This would have been particularly important for our tree-based ancestors.

A fingerprint works on the same principle as a car tire. In wet conditions, the ridges on both a tire and a fingerprint channel water away from the gripping area to allow better traction.

WHY DO PEOPLE SHIVER?

A person who is cold, excited, or afraid will sometimes shiver, involuntarily tensing the muscles to generate heat and produce a warming, calming effect. Shivering is a reflex action to keep the body warm and safe.

Shivering generates heat because it involves vigorous muscular contractions, which create warmth by expending energy. Shivering can use up to 400 calories per hour.

Shivering occurs only in warm-blooded animals, usually as a response to cold. If the core body temperature drops to an unacceptable level, the nervous system signals the brain to trigger the shivering reflex, first to protect the vital organs and then to warm the extremities.

Shivering can also occur when a person is excited or afraid. In these situations, the nervous system sends messages throughout the body that stimulate the muscles, resulting in shivering.

WHAT IS THE DIFFERENCE BETWEEN HARD AND SOFT WATER?

Soft water is water that contains low levels of minerals. Generally speaking, rainwater is naturally soft. As it permeates the ground and enters water reservoirs, it picks up various minerals, making it hard. Although hard water contains other metals, it usually has high levels of the metal ions calcium and magnesium.

Soft water increases the effectiveness of soaps and detergents. When mixed with soft water, soap provides a rich and creamy lather not found when it is mixed with hard water. Soft water is far more efficient than hard water and requires less soap. Cleaning with soap and soft water is also faster because the metal ions in hard water form insoluble salts, resulting in scum. The cleaning difficulties associated with hard water are the reason for its name. Soft water also results in far fewer limescale deposits in household items such as kettles and washing machines.

Despite its inconvenience for cleaning, hard water contains essential minerals and is considered better for drinking. Some studies show a reduced level of heart disease in men who drink hard water. The calcium in hard water is also beneficial for teeth. The minerals alter the flavor of the hard water, making it more palatable. For this reason, hard water is used to make certain beers and whiskeys. The minerals in some hard waters also stop corrosion and can help prevent damage to underground pipes.

Some water can be softened by filtration or by reducing the mineral levels through other means. Boiling can soften water if its (temporary) hardness is caused only by bicarbonate ions.

WHAT MAKES A PERSON GOOD-LOOKING?

Certain people are deemed by society to be good-looking. Although beauty is in the eye of the beholder, studies show that some universal factors contribute to physical beauty.

One of the most important factors of beauty is symmetry. A face that is perfectly symmetrical is generally found to be good-looking. Symmetry is a sign of health and a sign that the person is free from disease or deformity. A so-called golden ratio has been discovered, whereby the various aspects of the face in good-looking people accord to the ratio of 1:1.618, which promotes symmetry. If the face has these proportions, it will usually be considered attractive. Similarly, bodily proportions play a role, with a hip-to-waist ratio in women of 0.7 (where the waist circumference is 70 percent of the hips) considered ideal. The proportion of body mass to body structure is another important determinant for both sexes. For both men and women, pronounced cheekbones and a strong jaw are also appealing as signs of health and strength. A clear and healthy complexion is also found attractive. And it is believed that a familiar face—

one that we are constantly exposed to—is considered more attractive as well.

Most other universal beauty indicators also relate to health and the ability to provide strong offspring. In men, an erect posture, a wide chest, and a greater-than-average height are important because they indicate physical strength (and an ability to produce and protect healthy offspring) and confidence. Well-defined muscles and some body hair are also often appealing to women, as they are signs of testosterone and masculinity. In women, a youthful appearance is important, and long fingernails and hair can also be signs of beauty. These attributes are thought to indicate health. Vivid lips, large eyes, dimples, and white teeth are also signs of health and beauty in women.

WHY IS THE COLOR YELLOW ASSOCIATED WITH COWARDS?

The color yellow has traditionally been associated with cowards. Even today, cowards are sometimes called yellow.

Yellow has had this connotation since the 1800s. The term "yellow dog" was used to describe cowardly people at that time, and the term "yellow belly" was used in American slang in the early twentieth century to describe a person who lacked courage.

It is not entirely clear why yellow was used to refer to cowards. Asians were known as the yellow race and the "yellow peril" from the late 1800s because of the perceived threat they posed to the West. But it is not widely believed that this had anything to do with cowardice.

The color yellow (although not the term) has been associated with treachery and cowardice for centuries. In France, the doors of traitors were painted yellow, and the yellow medieval star branded the Jews as having betrayed Jesus. Paintings of Judas, the Apostle who betrayed Jesus, show him wearing yellow robes. Additionally, victims of the Spanish Inquisition wore yellow. A yellow flag was a symbol of quarantine for victims of yellow fever, and the term "yellow journalism" (which employed sensational headlines) dates to the 1800s.

Although any of these could be the origin of the color's association with cowardice, a more compelling theory is from a principle of medicine dating back to the Middle Ages that there are four humors, or fluids, in the body, which determine a person's physical and mental health. It was thought that if any of the humors became imbalanced, ill health would result. The four humors are blood, phlegm, black bile, and yellow bile, and it is yellow bile that makes a person irritable, choleric, and liable to act irrationally.

WHAT IS THE ORIGIN OF THE RED AND WHITE BARBER POLE?

For years a barbershop has been signified by the red and white striped pole standing in front of it.

The origin of the colors of the barber pole is said to be the bloodletting service that barbers once performed. In the Middle Ages, before professions became specialized, barbers played various roles, including dentist, surgeon, and bloodletter.

Bloodletting was a popular medical practice for centuries and involved withdrawing large quantities of blood from a patient in the hope that it would cure the patient of disease or prevent illness. A barber's patients would tightly grasp a pole to swell their veins, and the barber would cut the veins to release blood. Once this was done, used bandages were draped around the pole to dry. The wind also made them twist around the pole, making a red and white spiral pattern. Leeches were also used to drain blood, and it is thought that  they were kept in a brass basin at the top of the pole, which is still sometimes seen today.

The red and white pole became a symbol for the barbershop and an advertisement for the types of services the barber performed. The traditional pole has persisted to this day.

Red, white, and blue poles appeared in parts of America, probably to replicate the colors of the national flag, although some suggest the blue represents venous blood and red represents arterial blood.

⁇ WHAT ARE "CROCODILE TEARS"?

Someone who cries "crocodile tears" is pretending to be upset. Crocodile tears are an insincere display of emotion. The expression has been around since the 1400s and is seen in the works of Shakespeare and Rudyard Kipling.

Crocodiles have glands in their eyes that produce a fluid to help lubricate their eyes if they are out of water for a time. These animals cannot actually cry because they lack tear ducts, but this lubricating secretion gives the appearance of tears.

These secretions in the crocodile's eyes are often present while the crocodile is eating its prey. This led to the ancient belief that the crocodile was crying for the victim that it was eating—obviously hypocritical tears. The crocodile tears— false tears—were also thought to be used to help lure the crocodile's prey before the crocodile killed it. It was these ancient beliefs that gave rise to the expression.

WHY DO GEESE FLY IN A V FORMATION?

When a flock of geese migrate, they generally fly in a V formation. Until recently, scientists could only guess why geese did this, but it is now known that there are a number of logical reasons for the behavior.

Many ornithologists believed that this form of flying conserves energy, but there was no physical evidence of this. Then a team of scientists attached heart monitors to a flock of birds. When flying in a V formation, it was found that the heart rates of the birds are much lower than when they fly solo. Flying in a V formation reduces the wind resistance for some of the birds and allows them to glide and conserve energy. This is because the lead birds break the air and create an uplifting draft. Similar to a team of bike riders, the lead birds regularly swap positions to recover, allowing other birds to take their place. Indeed, it has been shown that birds can fly 70 percent farther when in a V formation than when alone.

Scientists also believe that geese fly in this way so that it is easier to see and keep track of the entire flock. This allows the geese to communicate during their long flights. Fighter pilots also use this technique to better see each other. In addition, because of where the eyes of the goose are situated on the sides of the head, if geese flew exactly behind each other, they would need to tilt their heads to the side to properly see the other geese. This would result in asymmetrical wing movements, which would not be as aerodynamic or as energy efficient.

HOW DID THE TERM *BOOTLEGGING* ORIGINATE?

Bootlegging refers to something that has been smuggled or acquired without the payment of taxes or royalties. Black market CDs and DVDs are typical bootlegged items these days—they are sold without the permission of the copyright holder.

The term was frequently used in the United States during the Prohibition era of the 1920s and '30s. During this time, when the sale of alcohol was not allowed, there was an enormous black market for illegal alcohol. Bootleggers smuggled alcohol into the country and sold it without any taxes having been paid. Bootlegging is different from moonshining, which is the practice of illegally selling homemade alcohol, sometimes known as "white lightning."

The term *bootlegging* has been in existence since the late 1800s and derives from the trick of concealing something illegal, often a bottle of alcohol, down the leg of a high boot. This practice is thought to have originated with pirates, who wore knee-high boots, which they used to conceal some extra booty for themselves instead of sharing it with the rest of the crew.

IS TELEKINESIS POSSIBLE?

Telekinesis (or psychokinesis) is the ability to move or influence the behavior of inanimate objects using only the power of the mind. It literally means "distant movement," and has been popularized in movies such as *Star Wars* and television shows such as *Charmed*. People sometimes question whether this "mind over matter" concept is physically possible.

Throughout history there have been reports of people moving objects with their minds. People who believe in and attempt to contact poltergeists have been said to move things without touching them, and other people have claimed to be able to levitate themselves or play musical instruments from a distance. These reports, however, are generally anecdotal.

Despite this, experiments conducted in the 1930s as to whether people could influence the throws of dice have lent some weight to the credibility of telekinesis. It was later shown that instead of the usual 50 percent hit rate with dice, subjects recorded a rate of 51.2 percent. Given the enormous number of trials involved, this differential was significant. A Russian woman, Nina Kulagina, also demonstrated levitation and the ability to move objects during the 1950s in front of worldwide audiences. More recently, Uri Geller displayed the ability to bend spoons and keys without touching them, most famously on a British radio show in 1973.

Skeptics claim that these people are adept magicians who use sleight of hand and other artifices, and to date, there have been no scientifically tested instances of telekinesis. As with most concepts that lack proven evidence, there is much conjecture and suspicion about it. That said, some psychologists claim that the laws of physics do not preclude telekinesis, and many psychics think that everyone has the ability to perform telekinesis. They claim that it is just a matter of relaxing, concentrating, visualizing, and focusing, although many agree that it takes years of practice before results are seen.

WHAT CAUSES "PINS AND NEEDLES" IN THE FEET?

Commonly referred to as "pins and needles," paresthesia is the abnormal burning, prickling, or numbing sensation sometimes felt in the feet, legs, arms, or hands. It is not normally painful and usually lasts only a short while, with symptoms reducing once the affected limb is moved around. Some people say that the particular limb "has gone to sleep."

Paresthesia is generally caused by placing pressure on a nerve through lying on it awkwardly. This blocks the sensory messages sent to the brain, and the result is numbness. The tingling sensation occurs when the pressure is released and the nerves begin sending signals to the brain again. Pinched nerves that are compressed can have the same effect. Lying on a limb can also reduce the blood supply by compressing the arteries, and this can also produce "pins and needles." This is more common in the elderly, who sometimes have poor blood supply to the limbs because of hardened arteries or arthritis.

Certain medications, excessive alcohol intake, vitamin deficiencies, and diseases such as diabetes or multiple sclerosis can also cause the condition. Nerve damage can result in chronic cases of paresthesia, which can sometimes be relieved by physiotherapy or surgery.

SHOULD YOU FEED A COLD AND STARVE A FEVER?

It's a commonly heard remedy: "Feed a cold and starve a fever." Many claim that this is a merely an old wives' tale that dates back to the 1500s. Some believe it originated with the idea that if a person was cold (with a chill), he or she should eat to increase internal heat, whereas the opposite was true when a person was overheated with a fever.

Most medical professionals have been trying to dispel this myth for years, claiming that a sick person should maintain normal eating habits and should not stress the body by either starving or gorging. Food is required for the body's metabolism to work properly, and starving makes it more difficult for the body to fight illnesses, such as fevers. Similarly, they say, a cold is a virus that cannot be cured by anything that we eat.

Despite doctors often disagreeing with the claim, there is now some evidence that eating and starving can help to ward off illnesses. A team of Dutch scientists conducted experiments that showed that after a meal, certain chemicals are stimulated in a person's body, and these act to increase the immune system and destroy infected cells. These chemicals help to destroy the viruses responsible for colds. Starved patients, on the other hand, were shown to have an increase in another chemical that helps to produce antibodies that fight the bacterial infections responsible for most fevers. Although these experiments lend weight to the notion of feeding a cold and starving a fever, researchers recommend that until more is known, people shouldn't change their eating habits whether they have a cold or a fever.

WHAT ARE THE HARMFUL SIDE EFFECTS OF COCAINE?

Cocaine is a highly addictive narcotic that is illegal throughout most of the world. It is an alkaloid that is obtained from the leaves of the coca plant, and it acts as a stimulant to the central nervous system, giving the user a

feeling of euphoria and heightened awareness. It is also an appetite suppressant.

In addition to euphoria, cocaine often results in restlessness and hyperactivity. Feelings

of euphoria are quickly replaced with depression and a craving for more of the drug. Hallucinations and paranoia are side effects produced by excessive usage.

Cocaine dramatically increases a person's blood pressure and heart rate. This can cause a condition called tachyarrhythmia, which can be life threatening, especially in people with a preexisting heart condition. Cocaine also results in an increase in muscular activity and heat production. Intense vasoconstriction also reduces heat loss (which is why many cocaine users perspire heavily), and this vasoconstriction can also cause muscle cell destruction and kidney failure. Additionally, snorting cocaine can result in the nasal cartilage degrading or disappearing altogether.

Cocaine use can lead to respiratory or heart failure, stroke, or hemorrhaging in the brain. Any one of these can cause death. In fact, cocaine users are thought to be seven times more at risk of heart failure than nonusers, and during the hour immediately after use, the risk is 24 times higher. Cocaine is said to account for 25 percent of the heart attacks in people ages 18 to 45.

There is no known antidote for a cocaine overdose.

WHAT IS THE DIFFERENCE BETWEEN HOLLAND AND THE NETHERLANDS?

The names Holland and the Netherlands are often used as synonyms, but this is not technically correct and causes consternation among the Dutch.

The name Holland derives from *holt land*, which means "wooded land," whereas the name Netherlands means "low land."

Holland is a region in the central west of the Netherlands, the latter being the full name of the country. The region of Holland is divided between two provinces of the Netherlands, North Holland and South Holland. These provinces were formed in 1840.

Holland is the cultural and economic center of the Netherlands and includes the major cities, such as Amsterdam. Centuries ago, Dutch merchants sailed from the ports of Holland to distribute goods around Europe. This resulted in many foreigners hearing of Holland before they heard of the Netherlands and so they used the former name to refer to the entire country. This tradition has continued in modern times.

 WHAT CAUSES DEPRESSION?

Although many people experience sadness and think that it constitutes depression, clinical depression is a health condition and more than simply a temporary state.

There are a number of brain chemicals called neurotransmitters, which allow electrical signals to be sent within the brain. The neurotransmitter serotonin helps regulate sleep, appetite, and emotion; dopamine is associated with pleasure and reward; and norepinephrine is associated with arousal and alertness. People with clinical depression have lower levels of these neurotransmitters. Antidepressant medications tend to increase the levels of these neurotransmitters in the brain. Although it is not known exactly why these levels are lower in depressed people, it is thought that some people inherit the condition while others have personality traits that are conducive to depression. Certain situations can also cause the neurotransmitters to become imbalanced, which leads to depression. Things such as persistent stress, difficult life events, and the loss of a loved one can cause this imbalance.

Certain illnesses, medications, drug or alcohol abuse, or a deficiency in vitamins are also known to cause depression. Some types of depression are also thought to occur during winter, when there is less sunlight, because the body produces more melatonin, which somehow causes depression.

Evolutionists claim that depression is a mechanism that can help people assess whether their goals are reachable and that it can lead people to accept a satisfactory, rather than perfect, outcome. These people are thought to live happier lives. In addition, if a person is vying to dominate a social group but is losing, depression can cause him or her to back down from an arrogant attitude.

WAS *THE STRANGE CASE OF DR. JEKYLL AND MR. HYDE* BASED ON A REAL PERSON?

Robert Louis Stevenson was inspired to write his famous book *The Strange Case of Dr. Jekyll and Mr. Hyde* by a respected businessman named William Brodie. The theme of the book is that the evil in every man can override the good. Brodie, born in 1741 in Edinburgh, was the son of a rich cabinetmaker. In fact, Stevenson's father had furniture made by Brodie.

Brodie was a trusted city councillor and deacon of the Incorporation of Wrights and Masons and while building cabinets for people, he installed and repaired people's locks and security systems.

By night, however, Brodie was a gambler and a thief. At age 27 he robbed his first bank, and for the next 18 years he continued with a clandestine life of crime. He used his daytime profession to help him gain access to the houses of the rich. He used his illegal money to maintain two mistresses, five children, and a severe gambling habit. Brodie recruited a gang of three thieves and in 1786 raided the Excise office on the Canongate, a street in London. One of his gang was caught and informed on Brodie, who was arrested while hiding in Amsterdam. He was taken back to Edinburgh, where copied keys, guns, and a disguise were found in his house. He stood trial in 1788, was found guilty, and was hanged on October 1 using gallows that had been designed and paid for by Brodie.

Some claim that Brodie bribed the hangman and wore a steel collar to prevent his death. Although there were rumors of him being seen in Paris later that year, it is more likely that he was buried, as reported, in an unmarked grave at the church in Buccleuch, a hamlet in Scotland.

WHAT CAUSES PEOPLE TO HALLUCINATE?

Hallucinations are a sensory perception (via any sense— taste, touch, sight, smell, or sound) experienced in the absence of external stimulus. The word is derived from the Latin word *ālūcinārī* meaning "to wander in mind."

Hallucinations are common, with around 40 percent of people reporting to have experienced one. The most typical types of hallucinations are hearing voices when no one has spoken, seeing lights or objects that aren't there, or feeling crawling sensations on the skin. Although early psychiatrists, such as Sigmund Freud, believed that hallucinations are a projection of the subconscious, most experts now agree that they are most likely caused by functional deficits in the brain and in some cases a lack of the neurotransmitter dopamine.

There are many potential causes of hallucinations. Certain drugs, such as LSD, "mushrooms," and ecstasy, can act as neurotransmitter mimics, changing the signals received by neurotransmitter receptors in the brain. This can result in an altering of the brain's sensory perception and cause hallucinations.

Psychotic disorders, such as schizophrenia, commonly produce auditory hallucinations, such as hearing voices, while lesions or injuries to the brain can also alter its functions and result in hallucinations. Severe medical conditions, including liver and kidney failure and brain cancer, can also cause them, as can bad fevers, post-traumatic stress disorder, and other serious or prolonged cases of stress. Physical and emotional exhaustion and sleep deprivation are other common causes, as they blur the line between sleep and consciousness. Sensory deprivation from deafness or blindness can also result in hallucinations, because it is thought that the brain is compensating for a lack of external stimulation.

WHAT ARE THE ORIGINS OF THE EXPRESSIONS "ON THE WAGON" AND "ONE FOR THE ROAD"?

The term "on the wagon" refers to refraining from drinking alcohol for a time while "one for the road" refers to one last drink before leaving, which will make the journey home more enjoyable.

One theory is that "on the wagon" derives from the water wagons in America's past before roads were paved. In order to keep down dust, horse-drawn water wagons would spray the streets. Anyone who had sworn off alcohol was said to have "climbed aboard the water wagon." Although this may be the origin of the phrase, there is another more colorful explanation, which relates to "one for the road" as well.

It is thought that in London in the days of public hangings, the condemned man would be taken through the town to the gallows on a wagon. Some say he was allowed one drink at every tavern on the way, so that he was drunk by the time he reached his place of death. At the last pub, he was given "one for the road" before he was put "on the wagon," never to drink again. Another theory is that he would be given only one drink along the way, while still another is that the driver would have "one for the road," and the prisoner, not allowed to drink, was "on the wagon." Others believe it was the prisoner who had "one for the road," while the driver was left "on the wagon."

HOW DID THE CUSTOM OF GIVING ENGAGEMENT AND WEDDING RINGS ORIGINATE?

In many parts of the world, it is tradition for a man to give a woman to whom he proposes an engagement ring. Then on the day of the wedding, he gives her a wedding ring. Sometimes the man also receives a wedding ring from the woman.

It is thought that the ring as a symbol of marriage may have evolved from an African custom of tying the bride and groom's wrists together with grass during the wedding ceremony.

The engagement ring was traditionally seen as an agreement to chastity and a future wedding. Before coins were minted in ancient Egypt, gold rings were used as currency, and some believe that an Egyptian man would place a ring on his new wife's finger to show that he trusted her with money. The engagement ring was generally worn on the fourth finger of the left hand. This is thought to date back to ancient Egypt, where it was believed that the "vein of love" is located at that finger. The early Greeks and Romans also gave rings and believed in the "vein of love," which is blood that runs from the fourth finger to the heart. By wearing a ring on this finger, a married couple declared their eternal love for each other.

Wedding rings were formalized by Pope Innocent III in 1215. He declared a longer period between the engagement and the marriage. An engagement ring adorned with gems or diamonds was given as a promise to marry, and a second, plainer ring, the wedding ring, was placed on the bride's finger during the wedding ceremony.

These traditions have continued to modern times.

WHY DO DOGS HAVE WET NOSES?

Dogs' noses are often wet, and people wonder why.

Folklore says that at the time of Noah's ark, two dogs were chosen by Noah to patrol the ark and check on the other animals. The dogs noticed a hole in the ark through which water was leaking furiously. One dog sought Noah for help, while the other blocked the hole with his nose, averting certain disaster. The wet noses of dogs were said to be a badge of honor from that time on to mark the valiant effort.

In reality, the main reason a dog's nose is wet is because dogs frequently lick their noses. When a dog is healthy and happy, it will lick its nose more regularly, which is why a wet nose on a dog is typically a sign of good health. When a dog is ill, it tends not to lick its nose as much, which results in a dry nose. However, some breeds of dog, such as bulldogs, have high-set noses, which they can't reach with their tongues. This means that their noses are generally dry. Cats and cows are also known to be frequent nose lickers, although the raspy tongue of the cat does not usually result in a wet nose.

Although nose licking is the predominant view, others believe that a dog's nose is wet because moisture evaporates through its nose, helping the dog to cool down.

WHAT CAUSES PEOPLE TO BE NEARSIGHTED OR FARSIGHTED?

Nearsightedness is an eye condition called myopia. It means that a person can see nearby objects while distant objects appear blurred. It is the most common eye problem, with about 25 percent of adults in the United States experiencing it. In nearsighted people, the eye is usually bigger than normal, and this makes the retina (which covers the back of the eye) stretch too thinly. This refractive defect in the eye means that light focuses in front of the retina instead of directly on it. The condition can be rectified by refractive surgery or by concave corrective lenses, which redirect the light on to the retina.

Farsightedness is called hyperopia (or hypermetropia). It is not nearly as common as myopia. It means that a person can see distant objects but not close ones. The person's eyeball is too small, making it unable to focus on nearby objects.

There is much conjecture about why some people have eye conditions and others don't. The most widely held view is that eye conditions are genetic. Research has identified the specific genes responsible, and hereditary testing for myopia has resulted in an 89 percent correlation between the genes and the eye condition. Others believe that environmental factors play a role. Some experts think that myopia is caused by a weakening in the ciliary muscle that controls the lens, making it unable to adjust the lens to see far distances. Because we focus on nearby objects most of the time by reading or typing a lot, the muscle is rarely used and becomes weak. Supporting this theory is the fact that in China, myopia is far more common in people with higher education. Because corrective lenses do the work of the ciliary muscle, some believe they make the muscle even weaker and increase the problem. Instead, they say, eye exercises to strengthen the muscle should be done. Others believe that diet and nutrition play a role in eye problems, with diets rich in carbohydrates leading to eye conditions. Evolutionists argue that people in cultures where little hunting occurred were more prone to myopia because seeing long distances was not as important as in cultures where more hunting occurred.

 **WHY DO VOLCANOES ERUPT?**

A volcano is a place where magma, ash, and gases come out of the earth, sometimes in a large eruption.

Because of the intense heat that exists deep within the earth, some rocks slowly melt and form into a thick, flowing substance known as magma. This substance is lighter and less dense than the solid rock surrounding it, and this causes it to rise to the surface. When the magma is near the surface, it will sometimes block hot gases from escaping. These gases expand and increase (as the magma cools, it releases more gases), and the pressure builds up under and within the magma. This can result in the volcano fracturing in an

eruption. Once the magma expels itself onto the surface, it is known as lava.

Some eruptions are more explosive than others. The explosiveness often depends on the density of the magma. If the magma is thin and watery, then the gases are able to easily escape from it, and the magma merely flows out of the volcano as lava. Thick magma, however, results in high pressure and often leads to an explosive eruption in which magma blasts into the air, breaking into pieces called tephra.

A violent eruption can have a devastating effect on the surrounding area, as can a slow lava flow, which often destroys buildings in its path.

Sometimes people are unaware that certain mountains are actually volcanoes. This is because centuries might pass between eruptions. Washington state's Mount St. Helens erupted in 1980 after lying dormant for 123 years.

WHAT CAUSES PARKINSON'S DISEASE?

Parkinson's disease is a degenerative disease of the brain discovered in 1817 by British physician James Parkinson. The disease is a chronic and progressive movement disorder, characterized by tremors, rigidity, slow movement, and difficulty walking. Depression and anxiety are also common.

The disease results from the degeneration of the brain nerve cells that produce dopamine. A neurotransmitter, dopamine stimulates the motor neurons that control the muscles. When dopamine is depleted, the motor system nerves are unable to control a person's movement or coordination.

The causes of Parkinson's disease are largely unknown. Genetic defects are thought to play a role, with the disease being inherited in certain instances. Most researchers, however, believe that the majority of cases are not caused by genetic factors alone. One popular theory is that the disease results from a genetic vulnerability to environmental toxins, such as those in some pesticides and industrial metals. Some think that certain toxins produce free radicals that inhibit dopamine production.

Many believe that head trauma causes Parkinson's disease; they cite the example of the great boxer Muhammad Ali, who has the disease. Most medical professionals, however, believe that such traumas can precipitate the initial symptoms of the disease but not actually cause it.

WHY DO WOMEN WEAR HIGH HEELS?

A high-heeled shoe is one that raises the heel of the foot significantly higher than the toes. (When both the heel and

the toes are raised, the shoe is called a platform shoe.) Women have worn high-heeled shoes for centuries, typically on formal occasions. Paintings from ancient Egypt depict women wearing high-heeled shoes as far back as 4000 BC.

A woman wears high heels because they enhance her beauty. High heels make a woman seem taller and change her posture. They make the calves appear more defined, as well as emphasize the femininity of a woman's walk by causing the buttocks to protrude and sway.

But high heels are often uncomfortable to wear, are difficult to walk in, and can cause damage to a woman's feet, ankles, and tendons. This means that many women have a love-hate relationship with high-heeled shoes.

❓ WHY ARE TYPEWRITER KEYS ARRANGED THE WAY THEY ARE?

The keys of typewriters are arranged in a specific fashion, with the letters QWERTY being the first six letters of the top row of letters. The 1874 Sholes & Glidden typewriters established the QWERTY layout, which had been patented by Christopher Sholes in 1868. The home row keys of ASDFGHJKL suggest that the QWERTY keyboard began as an alphabetical design and developed from there. Sholes originally experimented with an array of different keyboard layouts, and there are several theories about why he eventually settled on the QWERTY design.

The QWERTY layout is generally considered inefficient because of the distance the fingers have to move to hit the most commonly used keys. Many believe this was done intentionally to slow the typist's fingers and keep the machine from jamming. The incidence of jamming was further reduced because commonly used combinations of letters were placed apart from each other. This prevented the typebars of the letters in these combinations from clashing with each other and becoming stuck.

QWERTY also attempted to alternate common letters within combinations between the typist's hands, so that, as one hand was typing the first letter of a combination, the second hand could be in place for the second letter, thereby increasing typing speed.

Because *typewriter* is one of the longest words that can be typed using a single row of the QWERTY keyboard (the top row), some suggest that the sales staff designed the layout so that they could quickly type the word to impress customers. But most experts think this an unlikely reason for QWERTY.

Although most of these potential reasons are inapplicable today, modern computer keyboards have maintained the traditional layout despite various attempts to introduce more efficient designs.

WHAT IS THE DIFFERENCE BETWEEN A KANGAROO AND A WALLABY?

Kangaroos and wallabies are indeed very similar animals. They are both marsupials that belong to a small group of animals known as macropods, a Greek word meaning "long foot" and referring to animals with larger hind legs than forelimbs.

Both kangaroos and wallabies are most active at night and have forward-opening pouches in which their young offspring sit. They are both native to Australia and Papua

New Guinea and use their powerful tails as a balancing device while hopping. They are herbivores, generally feeding on grass and roots.

There are 45 species of kangaroo, which includes wallabies, and the only real difference between the two is that kangaroos are larger than wallabies. A macropod that isn't considered large enough to be called a kangaroo is called a wallaby. So wallabies tend to have a smaller and stockier build, with a shorter tail. Their hind legs are less powerful, making wallabies slower than kangaroos.

Wallabies usually live in thicker woodlands or rugged areas, while kangaroos tend to be on open plains, which are more suitable for hopping longer distances.

Kangaroos and wallabies are the only animals to use hopping as a means of travel, and large kangaroos can reach speeds of 43 miles per hour. The life expectancy of the average kangaroo is around 18 years. Male kangaroos or wallabies are known as bucks, boomers, or jacks, and females are known as does, flyers, or jills. The young of both kangaroos and wallabies are known as joeys.

WHAT ARE THE ORIGINS OF THE ENGLISH LANGUAGE?

English is the second-most-spoken language in the world, with an estimated 700 million people able to speak it.

It is a Germanic language of the Indo-European family and can be traced to three Germanic tribes who arrived in the British Isles during the AD fifth century. Before this time, a Celtic language was spoken, but this became largely unused (with speakers moving to Wales, Ireland, Cornwall, and Scotland) when the Angles, Jutes, and Saxons came from northern Germany and present-day Denmark. The Angles originated in Engle, where their language was Englisc, from which the word *English* derives.

Over the next few hundred years, different dialects of English evolved, and by the 900s, West Saxon, one of these dialects, became the official language of Britain. Old English came from this time, with Latin being brought from Ireland by the Christians. The language consisted of Anglo-Saxon, with some words from Danish, Norse (because the Scandinavian Vikings invaded Britain), and Latin. Invasions by the Normans in the eleventh century contributed French to the language. It is thought that because the English underclass cooked for the Norman upper class, words for domestic animals, such as cow, deer, and sheep, are English, whereas the meat from them, such as veal and venison, are French.

The Norman influence led to the development of Middle English, and by 1400, with the ascension to the throne of a native English speaker, King Henry IV, the dialect of London had emerged and become standardized. Modern English began around 1600 at the time of William Shakespeare, who is said to have contributed more than 1,500 words to the language. The English vocabulary is now the largest of any language worldwide.

❓ HOW DID THE GAME OF SOCCER ORIGINATE?

Many soccer-like games have been played throughout the world for thousands of years, any one of which might have been the origin of the popular modern game.

It is generally believed that the oldest game resembling soccer dates to the Han dynasty in China in 200 BC. A military manual from that time describes a game called *tsu chu* or *pinyin* in which a leather ball is kicked through a hole in a piece of silk cloth attached to two poles. It is thought that this was done for the amusement of the Chinese emperor, and the game may well have predated the military manual.

In Japan from around AD 600, a similar game was played called *kemari*, in which a number of players stood in a circle and kicked a ball to each other, trying not to let it hit the ground. The ancient Greeks and Romans also played games in which balls were kicked.

Indeed, most indigenous peoples around the world played games akin to soccer. In Canada and Alaska, the Inuit Eskimos played *aqsaqtuk*, where teams faced each other and attempted to kick a ball past the other's line, and the Native Americans played *pahsaheman*, another similar game.

Although any of these ancient games could have been the forerunner of soccer, modern-day soccer is said to have evolved from games in Western Europe and England. A similar game, known as *choule*, was played in France and is thought to have been taken to England with the Norman conquest, and in the Middle Ages, Shrovetide soccer games were played in Europe and England.

🄯 DOES CHAMPAGNE MAKE PEOPLE DRUNK FASTER?

It is commonly believed that people who drink champagne tend to get drunk faster than people drinking other alcoholic drinks at a similar pace. Those who imbibe the bubbly say that champagne goes straight to their head, making them light-headed and giggly.

A number of studies now show that there is a basis for this belief and that champagne does in fact get people drunk faster than wine does. In one study, people drank champagne on one day and on another day drank the same amount of champagne with the bubbles removed. At the end of the bubbly champagne session, the drinkers' alcohol levels were significantly higher than after the bubble-free session. In addition, after the bubbly session, the drinkers had more difficulty recognizing sequences of numbers, and their peripheral vision was more impaired.

Although experts are not certain about the reason for this phenomenon, it is generally believed that the bubbles in champagne speed up the absorption of the alcohol by the digestive system. Normally, 20 percent of the alcohol people drink is absorbed by the stomach, and the remainder is absorbed by the intestines. It is thought that somehow the carbon dioxide in the bubbles speeds the flow of the alcohol into the intestines and then into the bloodstream. Scientists believe that wine mixed with fizzy water would have a similar effect.

One way to reduce the effects of champagne is to drink it from a shallow glass. The larger surface area of the glass causes the bubbles to break and allows them to dissipate more quickly compared with a slender champagne flute, which tends to preserve the bubbles.

WHAT IS AMNESIA AND WHAT CAUSES IT?

Amnesia is a condition in which a person's memory is impaired. There are a number of different types of amnesia. In retrograde amnesia, a person is unable to recall prior events, while in anterograde amnesia, events after the amnesia are not committed to the long-term memory. Another type, traumatic amnesia, is when a person cannot remember for a transient period, and in lacunar amnesia, memory of a specific event is lost.

There are a number of potential causes of amnesia, and they are usually functional or organic. Organic causes are common and include damage to the brain because of disease or head injury. The more severe a head injury, the more serious the amnesia. Infections that affect the brain, such as herpes, can also cause memory loss, as can malnutrition or drug or alcohol abuse. In these cases, the brain often lacks vitamin B1, and brain cells are killed and cannot be replaced. If injury occurs or brain cells are killed in the area of the brain that deals with memory, amnesia can result. In the case of an injury, the memory can sometimes resume as the brain heals itself. Amnesia is also often a symptom of a degenerative brain disease, such as Alzheimer's disease.

Although many organic causes are accepted, it is the functional causes of amnesia that are the subject of debate. These are psychological factors, such as defense mechanisms. Some medical professionals claim that the brain blocks out traumatic incidents so as to reduce the conscious stress the person suffers. In childhood amnesia, people are unable to recall events from their childhood. Freud attributed this form of amnesia to sexual repression. There is still much conjecture about whether psychological factors play a role in amnesia.

❓ HOW DOES A TASER GUN WORK?

A Taser gun is a nonlethal electroshock weapon used to subdue a person with an electric shock. Designed in Arizona by Jack Cover in 1969, the name Taser stands for Thomas A. Swift's Electric Rifle. Taser guns are often used by the military and police, or sometimes by civilians for self-defense.

The gun works by shooting an electrical charge with high voltage but low current. A person's nervous system works by sending electrical currents throughout the body. A Taser gun interrupts and confuses the nervous system. The person's brain receives mixed signals, and this results in temporary paralysis. A Taser gun can also cause random muscles to spasm in the body, incapacitating the victim.

Also called stun guns, most models have two pairs of metal electrodes, which are charged by batteries. They include an oscillator, which fluctuates current to produce a pulse pattern of electricity. A built-in capacitor builds up charge and releases it to the electrodes. Some types of guns fire small, spearlike electrodes, which are attached to the gun with wires.

Like an air rifle, a stun gun is propelled by a charge of gas. The range of most stun guns is around 10 meters.

A Taser gun has high voltage, so as to penetrate the charge through the skin and into the person's body, but the current is low to avoid serious injury. Although a Taser gun is considered nonlethal, it can sometimes kill by disrupting the rhythm of the heart muscle. Other injuries can involve nerve damage or burning where the electrodes touch the skin.

❓ DID THE LOST CITY OF ATLANTIS EXIST?

The lost city of Atlantis is fabled as a utopian city that was destroyed in ancient times. The Greek philosopher Plato described it in 360 BC as a city of wealth, natural beauty, and an advanced civilization. He said that it flourished for nine thousand years before being destroyed by an earthquake and a tidal wave. Scholars have searched for it for centuries, with much debate as to where it lies, if anywhere. It has been placed near Cuba; Devon, England;

Antarctica; and Indonesia. Some place it in the middle of the Atlantic Ocean.

Thought by many to be merely a mythical island, Plato claimed it was somewhere west of the Pillars of Hercules, which are the Straits of Gibraltar. The only accounts of the city are in Plato's *Timaeus* and *Critias*, where he says that "in a single day and night of misfortune, the City of Atlantis fell into the sea."

Interest in Atlantis began in earnest in 1882, when books were written about it. This interest continued to modern times, and in 1938, leading member of the German Nazi Party Heinrich Himmler organized a search for it. No conclusive evidence was ever found for the existence of the city, with many believing that Plato's story was derived from mythology.

However, fairly recent research reported by an archaeology journal called *Antiquity* claims that Atlantis might lie in a salt marsh region off Spain's southern coast, near the port of Cadiz. The report is based on satellite images showing ancient ruins that appear to match Plato's descriptions. Two rectangular buildings surrounded by concentric circles can be seen, and these accord with what Plato said. Plato also claimed that the diameter of the largest circle was 5 kilometers, and the satellite images show that it is in fact between 5 and 6 kilometers. Some experts now believe that thousands of years ago, rising waters may well have submerged the city, not in one day as Plato suggests, but over hundreds of years. More research will still have to be done to convince the many skeptics, but it seems that the lost city may have existed after all.

❓ WHY DO SOME BRITISH PUBS ADVERTISE THAT THEY ARE A FREE HOUSE?

A number of pubs in Britain have a sign reading "Free House." There is a logical reason for this.

Pubs in Britain fall into one of three categories. A managed house is a pub owned by a large brewery and managed by an employee of the brewery, who is paid a wage. A tenancy is a pub is owned by a brewery but leased to a person, who pays rent to the brewery and buys all the beer from that brewery. These pubs are "tied" to a particular brewery. The third category is the free house, which often displays a sign signifying its status. A free house is a pub owned by a person who is not  tied to any brewery. Because a free house is independently owned, the owner can buy beer from anywhere and he or she keeps all the profits.

Free houses are usually very expensive to buy, with many pub chains, such as J. D. Weatherspoon, being free houses. Free houses are sometimes thought to sell beer more expensively, but this is incorrect. As they operate in the free market, they are often able to source beer from different breweries at cheaper prices.

❓ WHY DO THE ENGLISH DRIVE ON THE LEFT SIDE OF THE ROAD AND AMERICANS ON THE RIGHT?

Around a quarter of the world drives on the left-hand side of the road, with the balance on the right. The left-side drivers are generally British or from the British colonies, with the United States and Europe typically driving on the right.

The reason that the British drive on the left is because of the prevalence of right-handedness. In ancient times, when violence was common, people needed to be ready to defend themselves. Driving on the left allowed people to easily use a sword against oncomers. In addition, right-handed people find it easier to mount horses from the left, and if the horse was on the left of the road, it was safer to mount and dismount toward the side of the road, rather than the middle, where other traffic was.

In the early years of British colonization of America, people drove on the left. However, in the late 1700s, teamsters began hauling farm products in huge wagons pulled by a number of horses. The driver sat on the left rear horse so that he could lash the rest of the horses with his right hand. So that oncoming traffic could be seen, these wagons were driven on the right side of the road. This is said to have occurred in France and its colonies as well. The French Revolution in 1789 also helped with right-side driving in Europe. Originally, the aristocracy drove on the left, forcing peasants to drive on the right. After the storming of the Bastille, embattled aristocrats drove on the right to keep a low profile. Napoleon Bonaparte is also said to have been left-handed and enforced right-hand driving in France and its colonies. Elsewhere in Europe, Hitler also ordered some countries that he annexed to drive on the right. It is thought by some that the French general Lafayette recommended right-hand driving to Americans during his help in the buildup to the American Revolution. It is also thought that Americans preferred right-hand driving to cast off any British connection.

Because American cars were designed to be driven on the right and were extensively exported, some countries were forced to drive on the right to accommodate the cars. The combination of these reasons means that today most of Europe drives on the right.

❓ WHAT CAUSES OCEAN TIDES?

The tides of the ocean come in and ebb out every day due to gravitational forces. The primary gravitational force that causes the rising and falling of the tides is the moon. Although the sun's gravitational pull is 179 times greater than the moon's, because it is much farther from Earth, the sun's tidal effect is only 46 percent of that of the moon's.

Because Earth is solid, it moves as one. But the surface water can move freely. The difference between the forces at Earth's center and at the surface determines the tides. When the moon is directly overhead, the water is closer to the moon and so is pulled more by the moon's gravity and rises. On the opposite side of Earth, which is farther from the moon, the pull is not as strong, so the high tide is not as large.

During one day, Earth rotates 180 degrees in 12 hours, while the moon rotates 6 degrees around Earth in the same time. This means that each coastal place has a high tide about every 12 hours and 25 minutes. During a full moon, the sun, moon, and Earth form a line. The combined tidal forces due to the positions of the sun and the moon make for larger tides during this time, known as the syzygy. A very high tide is called a spring tide (from the German word *springen* meaning "to leap up"). In the first and third quarters of the moon, the sun and moon are at 90 degrees to each other, and they cancel each other out, resulting in smaller, or neap, tides.

The difference between the high and low tide at any given place is caused by the configuration of the ocean floor and the coastal shore. For example, the Bay of Fundy on the coast of Canada has the largest tides in the world because of the shape of the bay. The difference between tides there can range to up to 50 feet (16 meters). On the other hand, the tides in the Mediterranean and Baltic Seas are less because of their narrow connections with the Atlantic Ocean.

DOES BIGFOOT EXIST?

Also known as Sasquatch, Bigfoot is reported to be a large, apelike animal that lives in the forests of the Rocky Mountains in Canada and the United States. Bigfoot is said to stand about 8 feet tall. It is covered with hair and walks upright on its two hind legs. Although sightings date back to the 1700s, Bigfoot became famous in 1958 when enormous footprints were found in Humboldt County, California.

Footprints have indeed persuaded many to believe in Bigfoot, with some experts arguing that such large, well-spaced prints would be difficult to fake. Tracks found in Washington state in 1969 also suggested that the creature's right foot was crippled. This accorded with a number of eyewitness accounts of Bigfoot's gait. Handprints found in 1970 depicted a large, apelike hand with many irregularities, unlike anything in human anatomy. Indeed, these contained distinct fingerprints common to primates, which law enforcement agencies described as very real. Tested hair samples were also found to not match any known animal species, yet had characteristics common to both humans and animals. However, DNA from all other hair and feces samples have been inconclusive and have not shown that they are from an unknown animal.

A 1967 film of Bigfoot was long considered the most cogent evidence, as the footage was clearly not a bear but an apelike creature walking upright. But a man named Wallace claimed to have been involved in making the film, which he called a hoax. In support of the film, though, is the fact that eyewitness accounts from many different people are strikingly similar, in their descriptions both of the animal and of the sounds that it makes.

Despite the array of evidence and sightings, most scientists remain unpersuaded of the Bigfoot phenomenon. Many attribute the sightings to hoaxes or ancient folklore from Native Americans that people want to believe. In addition, there is a lack of fossil evidence, despite there being plentiful fossil evidence of prehistoric bears, cougars, and mammoths. Many experts think the sightings are merely of bears, and, in fact, in 1997, an Italian mountaineer claimed to have come face-to-face with Bigfoot and eventually shot one. It turned out to be an endangered Himalayan brown bear that is able to walk upright.

WHAT HAPPENS WHEN A PERSON IS IN A COMA?

A coma is a state of unconsciousness. The word comes from the Greek word *koma* meaning "deep sleep." A coma patient is alive but is usually unable to move or respond. As a coma deepens, the brain becomes less responsive to pain or any other factor and the less likely it is that the patient will come out of it.

Comas are to be distinguished from brain death, in which all brain activity ceases. A brain-dead person is unable to breathe, whereas a coma patient often can. A coma is also different from a state of vegetation, which may follow a coma. In a vegetative state, a person has usually lost environmental awareness but still has noncognitive functioning. Schizophrenia and catatonia can sometimes result in comatose-like behavior, but these too are different conditions.

A coma can result from a variety of causes. Central nervous system diseases and drug and alcohol intoxication are common causes. Diffuse pathologies are responsible for around 60 percent of cases. These include head trauma and intoxication. Expanding lesions and vascular problems can also result in a coma.

Comas typically last a few weeks, and people usually "wake up" progressively over a number of days. Whether a person comes out of a coma depends on the severity of the damage to the brain, and people who come out often exhibit physical, psychological, or intellectual problems. Recovery is usually gradual.

Debate rages as to whether coma patients should be kept alive for extended periods on life support.

CAN OUIJA BOARDS BE USED TO CONTACT SPIRITS?

A Ouija board is a device that people use to communicate with spirits during a séance. The board is covered with numbers, figures, and symbols. Participants place their fingers on a small wooden tablet called a planchette, which then moves around the board to spell out messages from spirits.

Many superstitions surround the use of Ouija boards and séances, but believers say that as long as a number of rules are followed, such as never playing alone, no harm can result. Others proponents think Ouija boards are a dangerous tool that should not be taken lightly because of the ability of inexperienced users to contact harmful spirits and demons. Some people have reported seeing ghosts and hearing voices during séances.

Skeptics do not believe that Ouija boards can contact spirits. Most psychologists think that participants make small, involuntary movements unconsciously and attribute them to paranormal forces. This is known as the ideomotor effect. It can be very powerful, and a person might find it impossible to be convinced that it is in fact his or her subconscious that is making his or her own hand move. Psychologists say that people often want to believe in the unlikely and are willing to trick themselves to this end. Other skeptics claim that the movements are caused by a manipulative participant who is trying to fool the other players. No scientific evidence has ever been presented to support the successful use of Ouija boards.

The name Ouija is from the French word *oui* and the German word *ja*, both meaning "yes." Ouija board is a trademark, although people often make boards by hand and use an overturned glass or a coin as the planchette.

HOW DO TELEPHONES WORK?

The standard household telephone is a surprisingly simple device that sends and receives sound over great distances. The word derives from the Greek words *tele*, meaning "far away" and *phone*, meaning "voice."

The phone contains three main parts. A switch connects or disconnects the phone from the public network when the handset is lifted or replaced. It also contains a small speaker, as well as a microphone.

When a person speaks into a telephone, the sound waves of the voice enter the mouthpiece. A transmitter behind the mouthpiece has an eardrum, which is a round metal disk called a diaphragm. The sound waves hit the diaphragm and make it vibrate at various speeds, depending on the variations in air pressure caused by the speaker's voice. Behind the diaphragm is a small cup filled with tiny grains of carbon. The sound waves change the resistance of the grains and modulate an electrical current flowing through the microphone. This electrical current then carries the sound to the telephone of the other person. The receiver at the other end is an electrical mouth and has vocal cords in the shape of another diaphragm. Again, it vibrates depending on the variations in the electrical current caused by the sound waves at the other end. These then hit the person's ear and the words are heard.

To speak on the telephone at your house to another person in his or her house, copper wires run from a box at your house to a box on the road. Cables then run to the phone company's nearest switch or to a box that acts as a digital concentrator and sends your voice down a single wire to the phone company. From there, it gets transmitted to another telephone. In times of the operator, when someone picked up a handset, the circuit would be completed, and current would flow between the house and the phone company. A bulb would light up corresponding to that person's house at the switchboard, and the operator would send a ring signal to the other party and then connect the two. Now the operator has been replaced by an electronic switch that makes the connection.

WHAT IS THE DIFFERENCE BETWEEN A HILL AND A MOUNTAIN?

There are no exact definitions to differentiate a mountain from a hill, and the two terms are often used to describe the same landform.

Generally speaking, a mountain is much higher and steeper than a hill. Although no set height exists for a landform to be classed as a mountain, some topographers consider a mountain to be any landform whose highest peak is at least 1,968 feet (600 meters) above mean sea level. Elevations above 984 feet (300 meters) are also considered mountains if they rise sharply from the ground. The average height of the world's mountains is about 1.25 miles (2 kilometers), with Mount Everest in the Himalayas being the highest at 29,029 feet (nearly 9 kilometers).

Another distinguishing feature is that a mountain usually rises more abruptly and has an identifiable summit, whereas a hill is a gentler elevation. A rocky face is also associated with a mountain, compared with a grass-covered hill. In addition, all the world's major rivers are fed from mountain sources.

Despite these explanations, the term that is used often depends on who named the landform and the prevailing local custom.

HOW DO SPIDERS SPIN WEBS, AND WHY DON'T THEY GET STUCK IN THEM?

A spider has two parts to its body, one of which produces silk. The silk is produced in glands in the abdomen and passed through tiny holes at the tip of the abdomen, which compress the silk. The silk starts in liquid form but immediately becomes solid when exposed to air.

A spider uses different glands to produce different types of silk. Sticky silk is designed to catch insects while stronger, nonsticky silk is used to tie down the web and for its frame. Still a different type of silk is used to build its cocoons. Some of the strands in a spiderweb are stronger than strands of steel of the same thickness.

Spiderwebs begin with a single thread, which is usually cast into the wind from a high vantage point. If the thread catches on to another branch, for example, the spider then walks along it and releases a looser thread below the first one and lays a number of anchor points. From there, the spider is able to spin its web.

The spider uses nonsticky silk to make the frame of its web and the threads that run out from the center. This is because the spider needs to walk along the structure to weave the rest of the web and to traverse the web generally. A spider also has legs that are covered in an oily coating that helps to prevent it from getting stuck  in its own web. But if a spider is startled and falls on to the sticky silk of its web, it is possible for the spider to become entangled in its own web.

WHAT IS FROSTBITE?

Frostbite is literally frozen body tissue. Medically known as *congelatio*, it usually occurs on the skin but can be deeper. It occurs when the skin is exposed to extremely cold temperatures for a prolonged period of time. With frostbite, the fluids in the body tissues and cellular spaces freeze and crystallize. This often damages the blood vessels, resulting in blood clotting and a lack of oxygen to the affected area. The hands, feet, nose, and ears are the areas most likely to be affected, with the early stages known as frostnip.

In addition to extreme cold, the factors of wet clothes, high winds, and poor circulation make frostbite more likely, and at times it can occur in as quickly as a few minutes. Children are at more risk than adults because they lose heat from their skin more quickly.

Frostbite is typically characterized by discoloration of the skin, which appears white and waxy, followed by burning or tingling sensations and then numbness and hardness. It can also result in intense pain. Frostbitten skin usually darkens after a few hours. As the area thaws, it becomes red and painful. If left untreated, frostbite can result in gangrene and amputation.

Frostbite should be treated by immersing the affected area in warm (not hot) water or by applying warm cloths. Unless the frostbitten area can be kept from refreezing, it is better to keep it frozen, as refreezing is likely to make tissue damage even worse. The area should not be massaged and should be moved as little as possible, and direct dry heat from a radiator or campfire should not be used to thaw frostbite. This can further burn the damaged tissue. Any blistering should not be disturbed, and warm drinks should be given to help heat up the person.

HOW DOES GENERAL ANESTHESIA WORK?

General anesthesia is used to make a person unconscious during surgical procedures. Amazingly, despite it being used for more than 150 years, scientists do not know exactly how general anesthesia works. The most commonly accepted theory is that it operates directly on the central nervous system to inhibit the transmission of brain signals. This results in a loss of consciousness, which affects a person's sensory awareness of factors such as pain. Another more specific theory is that general anesthesia inhibits excitatory neurotransmitters, such as acetylcholine and glutamate, and enhances inhibitory neurotransmitters, such as gamma-aminobutyric acid (GABA) and glycine. However, scientists do not know how anesthesia achieves this, except that it somehow alters the flow of sodium molecules into nerve cells. This lack of sodium is thought to prevent nerve impulses from being generated, which renders the brain unconscious.

In addition to acting on different areas of the brain, anesthesia works at the spinal cord to relax the muscles. Nerve impulses that would normally cause a muscle to contract are prevented from reaching the muscles. The muscle relaxation also causes paralysis of the respiration muscles; this means that artificial respiration must be administered.

Anesthesia causes a loss of consciousness that is different from deep sleep. In sleep, some parts of the brain speed up while others slow down. With anesthesia, however, the loss of consciousness that a person experiences is far more widespread. Local anesthesias, on the other hand, operate by blocking nerve transmission near the site of injection only, causing it to become numb. Otherwise, the patient is alert and aware.

IS THERE LIFE ON MARS?

Whether there is life on Mars is a question that scientists have speculated about for centuries. The obsession with life on Mars is probably because of its relatively close proximity to Earth and also because of the similarities between the two planets. In the 1600s, polar ice caps were observed on Mars. By the 1800s, astronomers knew that the length of a day on Mars is similar to the length of a day on Earth. Its axial tilt is also similar to that of Earth, meaning that seasons exist on Mars. H. G. Wells's 1897 book *The War of the Worlds*, which describes an invasion by Martians, also fueled the speculation.

In the past century, scientists observed that Mars is an arid land, exposed to harsh cosmic radiation because of its lack of a shielding magnetic field. These factors lent weight to there being no life on Mars. However, speculation has increased in recent years, owing to a number of significant findings. Evidence of water under the surface of Mars has been discovered, and in March 2004, NASA concluded that Mars was once a wet planet, capable of sustaining life. An orbiting probe near Mars then discovered methane gas in the Martian atmosphere. Methane could not last for more than a few hundred years without being replenished, and could be formed only by volcanic activity or by a life-form metabolizing hydrogen and carbon dioxide to produce methane (on Earth, organisms called methanogens do this). No volcanoes have been discovered on Mars, and in 2005, a group of scientists from the European Space Agency reported that the methane was of organic origin, suggesting life on Mars. At the conference where these findings were reported, 75 percent of delegates agreed that life once existed on Mars, and 25 percent believed that there is still life on Mars today.

Shortly after methane was found in the atmosphere of Mars, ammonia was also found. Ammonia would disappear within hours if it were not replenished. It is a compound of nitrogen and hydrogen, and although nitrogen is rare on Mars, no life can exist without it. This has led more scientists to believe that there are currently life-forms on Mars.

Photo Credits

All interior photos are from www.shutterstock.com; individual photographers are as follows:

page 1: © Trudy Simmons

page 2: © ChrisVanLennepPhoto

page 4: © lenetstan

page 5: © vadim kozlovsky

page 8: © Heath Johnson

page 10: © Joshua Resnick

page 13: © bluedogroom

page 17: © NicoElNino

page 19: © Patryk Kosmider

page 22: © ORLIO

page 26: © dien

page 28: © Pressmaster

page 31: © ags1973

page 33: © Kamil Macniak

page 35: © Oscar Moncho

page 38: © LaCameraChiara

page 41: © Vishnevskiy Vasily

page 44: © Dmitrij Skorobogatov

page 46: © IxMaster

page 48: © revers

page 50: © Amadeo AV

page 51: © Carolina K. Smith MD

page 53: © Kanea

page 54: © dangdumrong

page 58: © Ehab Edward

page 62: © TTstudio

page 64: © Maria Dryfhout

page 67: © hamdan

page 71: © ArTono

page 74: © Pavelk

page 76: © MaxyM

page 81: © telesniuk

page 84: © chrisbrignell

page 86: © Stkete

page 90: © Lestertair

page 95: © Josemaria Toscano

page 98: © Curioso

page 102: © somrak jendee

page 104: © prudkov

page 108: © somchaij

page 111: © dabjola

page 112: © Christian Musat

page 118: © Kuttelvaserova Stuchelova

page 121: © michelaubryphoto

page 124: © Maros Bauer

page 129: © ben smith

About the Author

Andrew Thompson divides his time between Australia and England. A lawyer by trade, his obsession with finding out the truth about aspects of the world that we take for granted has led him to accumulate a vast body of knowledge, which he has now distilled into book form.

See all of Andrew's books at www.andrewthompson writer.co.uk or at Twitter @AndrewTWriter.